RELATIONAL LEADERSHIP
A Biblical Model for Influence and Service

RELATIONAL LEADERSHIP
A Biblical Model for Influence and Service

Walter C. Wright, Jr.

PATERNOSTER

First Published in 2000 by Paternoster Press
Reprinted 2001, 2002 (twice), 2003 (twice), 2004, 2006
12 11 10 09 08 07 06   14 13 12 11 10 9 8

Paternoster Press is an imprint of Authentic Media
9 Holdom Avenue, Bletchley, Milton Keynes, Bucks, MK1 1QR, UK
285 Lynnwood Avenue, Tyrone, GA 30290, USA
OM Authentic Media, Medchal Road, Jeedimetla Village,
Secunderabad 500 055, A.P.

www.authenticmedia.co.uk/paternoster

Authentic Media is a division of Send the Light Ltd., a company limited by guarantee
(registered charity no. 270162)

British Library Cataloguing in Publication Data
A catalogue record for this book is available from the British Library

ISBN 0-85364-996-0

Cover Design by Mainstream, Lancaster
Typeset by Saxon Graphics Ltd, Derby
Printed in Great Britain by Bell & Bain Ltd., Glasgow

Contents

To the board, faculty, staff and students of Regent College
who gave me the space to lead while serving them.

Foreword

We begin by following. There are no 'born leaders'. We start out by following our parents, our siblings, older children in the neighbourhood. Later we follow teachers, coaches, bosses, managers, counsellors and guides. Eventually, writers and saints, preachers and prophets, some of them long dead, enter our lives as leaders and we follow.

And then somewhere along the line, whether we intend it or not, whether we want it or not, whether we realize it or not, people start following us. We become leaders. All of us. People see what we are doing and where we are going; it looks like we know what we are doing and where we are going. They follow. We are leaders before we know how to be leaders.

For some of us this is exhilarating. Leadership is a position of power; it is a place of prominence, we are looked up to, we are respected. We find we like being in charge; we like being followed – it increases our sense of worth, of importance. We look for ways to increase the power and use those who are following us to help us become what we want to be, to do what we want to do.

For others of us this is scary. Leadership is a position of responsibility; others are looking to us for guidance. If we say or do the wrong thing we are going to hurt people and if we get too involved with them they may well hurt us. We find we don't like being in charge; we don't like being followed – it interferes with our autonomy and our privacy. We look for ways to avoid the responsibility and have as little as possible to do with those who are following.

When we realize that we are inevitably all leaders in some degree or other, that 'leader' is not a role confined to a job description, we know that we need help. For being a leader, whether in prominence or in obscurity, can fuel our ambition and a lust for power that ends up using people and organizations to enhance oneself. It is tempting to lead by coercion or manipulation and end up valuing followers primarily as a means to further my strategies and goals. Or leadership can frighten us into withdrawing into a privatized isolation; we distance ourselves from others and their need for love and compassion and justice, separating ourselves from the people who follow us. We end up leading by remote control, perceiving followers as irritants and a bother. We avoid them. And when we can't avoid them, we condescend to them.

Without wisdom, without intelligence, and without vigilance, being a leader can diminish or even destroy us and the people around us. Being a leader so easily and so often depersonalizes us and those around us, making us less instead of more. Leaders of every shape and kind – mothers and fathers, friends and neighbours, brothers and sisters, presidents and chairpersons, pastors and teachers, artists and athletes – which is to say, all of us, need help. The track record of leaders through the centuries, whether in politics or business, whether in education or religion, whether in family or community, is not encouraging. The seductions and pressures of unmentored leadership can easily ruin us. Yes, we need help.

Walter Wright has been paying attention to the nature of leadership for a long time and offers timely and seasoned help. He has thought, taught, prayed, conversed, and read widely and deeply in and outside the Bible on the nature of leadership and has worked what he has learned into his own life. And now he writes. Leadership, as Walt Wright lives and writes about it, is not a role, not an assigned position. Leadership is a way of living that suffuses everything we do and are. Leadership is a way of being in the family and marriage, a way of being among friends, a way of going to work, a way of climbing mountains, and, most centrally, a way of following Jesus – all of which things he both does and reflects upon.

Eugene H. Peterson
Professor Emeritus of Spiritual Theology
Regent College, Vancouver, B.C.

Introduction

Leadership – What is it? How do you do it? Who is a leader? Who is not? For over thirty years I have been trying to understand the answers to these questions because I keep finding myself in situations where someone expects me to be one (a leader) and know what it (leadership) is.

Two years ago, I was asked to give the Earle Douglas MacPhee Address for the closing ceremony of the 78th Banff School of Advanced Management. What does one say to a group of veteran executives who have just spent four weeks intensely studying leadership with some of the finest faculty in Canada? As they prepared for the transition back into their corporate settings around the world, it seemed appropriate to talk about the relational nature of leadership. Leadership is a relationship between a leader and a follower – ideally, a relationship of shared vision, shared responsibility and shared leadership. So I prepared my remarks from the perspective of the people who look to them for leadership – the people in their organizations for whose success they are responsible. The title as published on the Banff School Web site was 'Look Out! – Here comes a Leader!' or 'Who are you? Who Cares?' Looking at a relational model for leadership, I focused on the character of the leader that adds value to the organization and contributes significantly to the shaping of the organizational culture. Who you are matters. What you believe and how that shapes your character does in fact make a difference to the people you lead. The relationships you build within your organizational setting deeply affect the way the organization's mission is carried out and the daily experience of those with whom you work. People do care who you are. It makes a difference. When the talk was posted on the Web, I received letters from a variety of sources affirming the importance of personal character and relationships. My thoughts must have been well received, because I was invited back the next year to give the closing address on the role of forgiveness in leadership.

This relational model of leadership has been evolving in my mind over the years as I work with people and work for people. Many of the foundational elements were forged without reflection while working my way through college as a ramp supervisor for International Flight Service, a contract service provider at San Francisco International Airport. There, with little authority, a low-paid team of short-term employees and tight airline schedules to meet, I learned the critical value of relationships. I could not do my job unless each member of my team did theirs and owned our overall objectives. Leadership was shared, responsibility was shared, even though I was accountable to senior management. And as a team we performed well and had fun together. That sentence probably sums up the governing philosophy of a relational approach to leadership: as a team we performed well and had fun together!

After college I had the privilege of working with and for some great leaders. Calvin Schoonhoven, Assistant to the President for Academic Affairs at Fuller Theological Seminary, believed in me and took a chance. With his encouragement I began to think about leadership within a Christian community. Glenn Barker, the Provost of Fuller, took me under his wing and became my mentor for twelve years, pouring into me the model of servant leadership that he embodied so well. David Hubbard, the brilliant president of Fuller, set a model of leader as theologian that still takes the measure of everything I do. And then there was Max DePree. Max DePree, former Chairman and CEO of Herman Miller, Inc., a Fortune 500 furniture manufacturer, author of *Leadership is an Art*, *Leadership Jazz*, *Letters to Zoe*, and *Leading without Power*, has probably shaped me more than any other single individual. When I was a young administrator at Fuller, Max was the chair of the Fuller Board of Trustees.

In 1981 I served as the founding director of the Institute for Christian Organizational Development at Fuller Seminary. Max DePree taught a course in leadership for us each year. As I watched and listened to him, and later read his books, I found a man who incarnated a deeply caring relational approach to leadership. By all measures of success, Max DePree has been recognized for his leadership at Herman Miller, and I watched him bring that leadership to the board of Fuller Seminary. This was a man of character whose deeply held Christian values permeated his relational approach to leadership.

With great audacity, when I became president of Regent College, I asked Max DePree to become my mentor – and he agreed. Now each year I have the marvellous privilege of spending one or two afternoons with Max reflecting on what I am learning, what I am trying to do, and drawing from his continually increasing wisdom on the subject of leadership. If there is any visible model for the leadership in which I would like to invest my life, it is the model of Max DePree at Herman Miller. Max integrated Christian beliefs with effective corporate leadership to make Herman Miller one of the most respected workplaces in America. He has become known as an outstanding relational servant leader. That is the standard against which I want to measure my growth as a leader.

This book is a work in progress. It is a reflection of my current thinking about leadership as I try to do it and teach it. For over thirty years I have been trying to live out my developing theological understanding of my Christian faith in a variety of roles in middle and top management. For over twenty years, I have been teaching classes and workshops on leadership, attempting to bring the best of contemporary thinking about leadership into dialogue with my own study in biblical theology. For the past eleven years, I have served as president at Regent College in Vancouver, British Columbia, and have found everything I have taught being put to the test.

In many ways I have been writing this book for thirty years. It forms the core of the course I teach, 'Leadership for Servants', but it keeps changing as new research and thinking is incorporated and new situations are confronted in the practice of leadership. The world around us keeps changing. Our organizations continue to change. The people we lead are changing. Leaders and leadership must change as well. Only God remains unchanged. And in Christian organizations, that is where it all starts.

In this study, I start with one biblical writer's critique of leadership in a first-century Christian community. The five sharp challenges raised by Jude's letter form the outline for the presentation of servant leadership that follows. Also, throughout the book, I try to ground the practical application of leadership in the wonderful biblical case study of Colosse. In this real-life, down-to-earth community of Christians, we watch relational leadership worked out in the midst of human emotion and organizational conflict. Building on the foundations laid in Jude and Colossians, I seek to set out a basic model of relational leadership as it has evolved from my reading and my daily efforts to exercise leadership in one particular Christian community. Many of my illustrations are drawn from my own experiences at Regent, at Fuller and in churches. While I apologize for the narrowness of this sample, it is the actual arena in which these principles and practices have been tested. This is not just theory. It is a way of leading that I am trying to live and to which I am prepared to be held accountable.

Leadership is a relationship, and for the rest of this particular journey, it becomes a relationship between you the reader and me as writer. May these thoughts and experiences stimulate your thinking about leadership and empower you to invest yourselves in the people for whose success you are responsible.

Chapter I

The Theology of Servant Leadership

This is a book about leadership, about biblical leadership, about servant leadership.[1] In these pages we will look at a model of leadership that starts with our relationship with God and moves out from there into relationships of service with those around us. It is a study of the theology and practice of servant leadership that takes as its starting point the book of Jude, which is a letter to Christian leaders.

What Is Leadership?

Before we begin this study, we need to clarify our definition of leadership. What is leadership? Who is a leader? Are we talking about the responsibility of people who hold positions of leadership in an organizational context, or are we talking more broadly in terms that include us all? Is every Christian a leader?

In the little book *I Heard the Owl Call My Name*, Margaret Craven tells the wonderful story of a young Anglican priest who does not know that he is dying of cancer. A wise bishop assigns him to the isolated and difficult parish of Kingcome, a Native American village in British Colombia. Mark Brian came to the village as vicar, thinking that his leadership was in his role, his position. Three years later he died in that village surrounded by a community of friends, knowing that his leadership was in his relationships and that he was led as often as he was followed. It was in his relationships with the village people that Mark was able to lead them, to make a difference in their lives. And it was these same relationships that enabled the village people to make a difference in Mark Brian's life and ministry. He taught them about the love of God. They taught him about the quality of life and the meaning of death.[2]

If by *leader* we mean one who holds a position of authority and responsibility, then every Christian is not a leader. Some are – some are not. But if by *leader* we mean a person who enters into a relationship with another person to influence their behaviour, values or attitudes, then I would suggest that all Christians should be leaders. Or perhaps more accurately, all Christians should exercise leadership, attempting to make a difference in the lives of those around them. This latter definition is the one put forward by the contemporary literature of leadership and management. In this study I will suggest that *leadership is a relationship – a relationship in which one person seeks to influence the thoughts, behaviours, beliefs or values of another person.*

In their classic text on the *Management of Organizational Behavior*, Paul Hersey and Kenneth Blanchard define leadership as 'any attempt to influence the behaviour of an individual or group'.[3] The same definition drives Howard Gardner's brilliant study of contemporary leaders, *Leading Minds*.[4] James MacGregor Burns, in his Pulitzer Prize–winning book *Leadership*, takes this one step further, arguing that transforming leadership is a relationship that raises the vision, values and aspirations of both the leader and the follower to new levels of expectation.[5]

> Leadership is about relationships that make a difference.

Jude and Leadership

On one of my recent rereadings of the New Testament, I came again to the book of Jude – a little letter right before the majestic and mysterious book of Revelation. Jude had never caught my attention in the past, but this time it jumped right off the page at me.

As one whose entire life seems to be entwined with leadership – trying to figure out what it means in my current role as a college president, and stopping occasionally to reflect and teach various topics in the area of leadership – I was amazed by the relevance of Jude's letter to the issues of leadership. These twenty-five verses form a powerful letter to Christian leaders today.

In this case, I do not mean only people who find themselves in positions of leadership – organizational executives, pastors, politicians. Jude is writing to the ordinary members of the church and warning them about some of their number who are seeking to influence the community, claiming to be leaders but in fact pointing people in the wrong direction. He is dismayed by the self-serving behaviour of some teachers who are seeking to provide leadership to the church. In the midst of that experience, he writes the powerful little letter we call Jude.

In particular, it was verses 12 and 13 that first captured my thinking. Jude describes the leadership of these false teachers in terms that Tom Peters, author of *In Search of Excellence* and *Thriving on Chaos* would use to describe the behaviour of what he calls 'non-leaders'.[6]

> [They are] shepherds who feed only themselves. They are clouds without rain, blown along by the wind; autumn trees, without fruit and uprooted – twice dead. They are wild waves of the sea, foaming up their shame; wandering stars, for whom blackest darkness has been reserved forever.

Five powerful images of the non-leader focusing on the use of power – images that will be central to this book. But before looking at these images, there are some other issues to be addressed, of which the first is, Who is Jude?

As I spent more and more time with this little book, I began asking people if they knew who Jude was. Most people did not. It is a book seldom referred to, and the average person could not tell you the content of the letter, let alone who the author was.

Jude introduces himself in verse 1 as 'Jude, a servant of Jesus Christ and a brother of James'. According to early tradition and most contemporary scholarship, Jude is assumed to be the younger brother of James and the brother or, if you will, the half-brother of Jesus.

I have a friend who is the third son in a successful family. His father is the president of a respected college; his mother is a published author; his oldest sibling is a very successful pastor of a large church; and the second sibling is president of another college in the USA. The father and both siblings have earned PhDs and growing reputations. My friend is a very talented and gifted man who now in his middle years has emerged as a nationally recognized Christian thinker and writer.

But as I watched him grow in the early years of his career, I saw an almost desperate need to live up to the expectations set by the other members of his family. He was driven to succeed. And succeed he has. I had no doubt that he would. His natural gifts and ability drew him into roles in which he continues to make important contributions. He is an established leader in his field and his reputation will continue to develop.

But in the early stage in my friend's development, I did not see his leadership emerging naturally and comfortably from his many gifts, but rather from his aggressive need to achieve, his need to live up to the model set by the other members of his family. He pushed himself and lived with a fairly strong sense of self-judgement. He seemed insecure as he measured himself against his family. At that stage in his life, I do not believe he was centred in his soul. From my perspective, as long as his leadership arose from his insecurity and his needs, it was less effective than it became when he relaxed and let it flow naturally from his many gifts and his dependence upon God.

Now, it's one thing to have older siblings who have PhDs and are successful leaders of churches and colleges. What if one brother was the head of the Jerusalem Church and the other the Saviour of the World! Where does that leave you?

That is where we find Jude. Jude who? The brother of James and the half-brother of Jesus. Third in line, at least, behind a family that he will never live up to. Maybe that is why I think it so wonderful that Jude starts his letter dealing with what I call the psychology of leadership, or better, the theology of leadership.

Prerequisites for Servant Leadership

Jude brushes quickly over his legitimate status as a 'brother of the Lord', identifying himself as a servant – a servant of Jesus Christ, and alluding to his status only in a secondary relationship to his brother James. In spite of the fact that as a brother of Jesus he would be accorded special recognition in the early church, he is anxious to point away from himself, something he criticizes the false leaders for not doing, and he moves immediately to his readers.

Centring

> To those who have been called, who are loved by God the Father and kept by Jesus Christ.

Jude here describes his readers in terms of three characteristics that I believe are prerequisites for leadership in the Christian community, three characteristics that set Christian leadership – the leadership of servants – apart from ordinary leadership. In fact, I believe Jude 1 addresses three critical questions that are foundational to any form of leadership anywhere:

- Who am I? Do I have worth? – dealing with the issue of identity.
- Will I be here tomorrow? – dealing with the issue of survival.
- Why am I here? – dealing with the issue of meaning.

Peter Koestenbaum, a secular philosopher of business, sees these three questions at the core of every leadership relationship.[7] In his book *The Heart of Business* he examines what makes an effective leader. He asks what gives a person the character that causes others to accept his or her influence – that enables the person to make a difference in the world.

Koestenbaum argues that effective leaders are centred in their souls. They have come to peace with the questions of identity, survival and meaning. It is this centredness that makes others listen to what they have to say, that gives them credibility. In their excellent book *Credibility*, James Kouzes and Barry Posner show that people follow leaders because they see a quality of character, a credibility worth trusting. People respond to this centredness, this quality of character.[8] To quote Koestenbaum:

> Centeredness is what makes people seem powerful, and its absence is what makes people perceive themselves and be perceived by others as ineffective and even impotent ... Centeredness is the source of authentic faith, belief and realistic self-confidence.[9]

Good words from a secular philosopher. So how do we get centred? How do we find that quality of character that people respond to? Look again at Jude 1.

1. Identity

In response to the question of identity, Jude answers that we are *loved by God*. Our value, our worth, our individual personhood is determined by the fact that God loves us, that he has entered into a relationship with us in which, out of his covenant faithfulness, he commits himself to our well-being, our growth and our eternal existence. Who am I? I am one known and loved by God. I am one of his. Our identity is not in our work or in our leadership. It is found only in the understanding that we are loved by God. This is key to leadership for Christians.[10]

2. Survival

As for survival, it does not matter whether or not we will be here tomorrow. Jude responds that what matters is that we are *kept by Jesus Christ*; or better, we are kept by God for the return of Christ. It is God who will keep us secure in and for Jesus Christ. The fears, the anxieties of today must fall into perspective before the truth that we are in the hand of God. Our life is shaped not by our positions or our accomplishments but by our relationship with God in Jesus Christ. Only that matters. Christian leadership is grounded on our relationship with God.

3. Meaning

And then there is the age-old question of meaning. Why am I here? Jude's answer is short. We are *called*. We have been chosen by God to be his people, to be his servants. What is the meaning, the purpose of my life? It is to be a child of God, to be his servant, to live my life for his glory and his honour. We are not called to a position or a role. We are not called to a specific ministry, lay or ordained. We are called to live the resurrected life in such a way that it points people to God wherever we find ourselves.[11] Leadership for Christians is about God, not about us.

Centredness is getting my life in perspective before God. It is knowing that I am loved, kept and called by God. Out of this identity, security and meaning comes a person of character – a person who is believed – a person who can influence others and make a difference in the world – *leadership*.

In his little book on leadership, *In the Name of Jesus*, Henri Nouwen argues that Christian leaders must find their identity deeply rooted in God's love,[12] and must realize that any valid leadership we seek to exercise must be grounded on a permanent intimate relationship with the incarnate Word, Jesus Christ.[13] This is an important little book and deserves to be read often by anyone who presumes to live out a role or responsibility of leadership. In this study, Nouwen captures well the three temptations of leadership that seek to draw us away from God: relevance, popularity and power. Only an intimate relationship with Jesus can anchor the Christian leader in the love of God.

This is the starting point for all who wish to exercise leadership as Christians, for all who seek to influence the people around them. We start by focusing on our relationship with God. We centre our soul in the hand of God – only then are we ready for leadership. Leadership for Christians starts with a vital relationship between the leader and God. This is the essence of Christian servanthood, of servant leadership.

I do not think this is easy, nor do I think it happens once for all. It is a continual process. As often as we reach out into the world trying to make a difference, we also need to be focusing on God, centring our soul. In recent years, the

media around the world have been filled with stories of
leaders whose uncentred lives have landed them in trouble
and tarnished their influence. But I do not have to look
beyond my own mirror to see fear, anxiety and insecurity.
The more I take on, the more I am conscious of my dependence upon God, my need for his presence at the centre of
my being.

Each of us must work out with God our own centring
procedure, our own way of investing in our relationship
with God in Christ. For me, there are five necessary
components:

Solitude: Time when I listen to God without distraction
               – ranging from praying alone in my room to
               walking a mountain trail in silence.

Study: Time for reflection on his Word – ranging from
               reading Greek in the library to reading Psalms
               by the seashore.

Worship: Time when I focus intentionally on the centre
               – the presence of Christ – with humble grati-
               tude, both in times of personal devotion and
               corporate communion.

Community: Time to celebrate shared relationships and
               balance uncentred lives with people who care,
               from family and friends to mentors and small
               groups, and

Ministry: Time to experience and share the love of God,
               to make a contribution, to exercise the gifts
               entrusted to me – to make a difference.

When the potter sits down to make something, she takes the
lump of clay and places it in the middle of the wheel. She
works patiently and intently to centre that lump of clay
before making any attempt to shape its future. Every potter
knows that if the clay is not centred, the vessel he or she
makes will be deformed. Even irregular, individualized pieces
must start with a perfect centring.[14]

This is true for each one of us who wants to make a difference in this world. The shape of our future leadership is determined by the quality of our centring.

Hesed

In verse 1, Jude started by focusing his readers on their relationship with God. Now, in verse 2, he shifts the focus onto our relationships with other people – our leadership. It is only out of centredness, out of an intimate relationship with God in Christ, that we can reach out in relationships and attempt to lead others, to influence the way they think and believe and act. Henri Nouwen calls this the solitude of the heart – a process that first attaches one's self to God, thereby empowering one's relationships with others.[15]

In my mind Jude 2 bridges the gap from living in the hand of God to walking in the world in relationships. Jude is writing to a community where some people are leading for their own benefit and dividing the community in a destructive fashion.[16] As Jude exposes these false teachers as a model of ineffective and dangerous leadership, he also gives us some clues to the character of servant leadership. What are the characteristics of servant leadership, of Christian relationships? I believe that Jude lists three in verse 2.

Mercy, peace and love be yours in abundance.

These are the characteristics of the leadership of people whose lives are centred in their relationship to God.

Jude 2 is easily passed over because it falls into the same category as 'Hello' and 'Dear Friend'. It is a greeting, a formal and almost common salutation. 'Mercy and peace' was the standard Jewish greeting of the day. It referred to the covenant kindness of God (*hesed*) and the shalom, or sense of total well-being, that flowed out of this experience of covenant faithfulness. Jude adds the word 'love' to his greeting, bringing Christian overtones into the leadership relationship. God's covenant kindness that results in peace or total well-being is most visibly modelled in the incarnation and sacrificial death of Jesus.

If we see this verse only as a 'dear friends' greeting, we will not spend much time with it. But it is more than a greeting. It is a prayer, an invocation that God will grant the readers an abundance of his mercy, his peace and his love so that it will overflow from their lives onto others. These three components of Jude's invocational greeting, I believe, represent three critical aspects of servant leadership.

Exercising leadership as servants involves love, peace and mercy. If we are going to be Christian leaders we need to be lovers, peacemakers and keepers of commitments. I only note these characteristics of the Christian leader in passing. They deserve to be unfolded and applied to our lives in detail. Yet as we move from our relationship with God to principles for leadership, we must acknowledge these three crucial elements of Jude's prayer so that we keep them always in the back of our mind.

- **Love** – we are to be lovers of people. Leaders must love the people for whom they are responsible, modelling the consistency of the love that God has poured out on us in Christ. Leadership is a relationship of love. It is an investment in the life of others for the purpose of their growth, their contribution and their walk with God. Only people who care about people will be effective leaders today.
- **Peace** – we are to be peacemakers. In a world of conflict, leaders bring calm. In a world of brokenness, leaders offer healing. In a world of loneliness, leaders provide relationship. Leaders work for the reconciliation and healing of relationships, for the creation of strife-free environments where people are freed to use the gifts they have been given and to grow. Leadership is a relationship of shalom, a relationship that works actively for the total well-being of those being led.
- **Mercy** – we are to be keepers of commitments. Jude uses the term 'mercy' in his greeting. This component

of Christian relationships, of servant leadership, may be the most important. When we hear the word 'mercy', we tend to think in terms of the English ideas 'pity', 'compassion', and sometimes, 'condescension' or 'undeserved', with a touch of our own pride thrown in. The Hebrew word *'hesed'*, which is translated as 'mercy', means much more than this.

Hesed, God's covenant love or covenant faithfulness, represents the commitment that God has made in his relationship with his covenant people – a commitment to be our God, to be there in our future, to be for us. That alone would be enough to elevate the importance of this word in defining our approach to leadership, but it carries even more content. *Hesed* is God's commitment to be our God even when we fail to live up to our part of the covenantal relationship. Even when we fail, God still commits himself to us and honours his end of the relationship by carrying our end also. That is where the 'mercy' comes in. We always fail. We cannot keep our end of the covenant relationship. We cannot live up to the requirements of being God's chosen people, his children, his servants. We try, and we fail. But God has committed himself to the relationship; he has committed himself to us in Jesus Christ and, because of his mercy, his covenant faithfulness, we can still be in relationship with God in Christ.

This is the model we have for being servant leaders who are full of mercy, who are keepers of commitments. It is promising to be there in someone else's future. It is committing ourselves now to be there in the future for another person, knowing that we and the other person will change between now and then. We commit to another recognizing the possibility, perhaps even probability, that they will not live up to our expectations. It means giving another person the space to change and committing to the person on the other side of change.

This is an important theme for Jude. Near the end of his letter, Jude calls on his readers to demonstrate this kind of commitment, to maintain their relationships with those who have been influenced by the false teachers, even with the false teachers themselves – to be there for them, accepting and caring for them personally even while patiently standing against the false teaching and dangerous leadership they represent.

Leadership for Christians means committing ourselves to be there in another's future as a friend, as one who cares, regardless of the circumstances that occur between now and then, regardless of the path our organizational roles may lead us.

Leadership is for lovers of people, peacemakers and keepers of commitment. These are not unique characteristics. Much of the current leadership research would also identify such qualities as important to leadership today. Yet because Jude grounds these characteristics of Christian servanthood in our relationship with God, he separates servant leadership from ordinary leadership – relationships with those we seek to influence are characterized by love, peace and *hesed*, mirroring what we ourselves have experienced in our relationship with God. Servant leadership is about a relationship with God that so shapes who we are that people see in us a person of character and commitment whose influence they choose to follow.

Is every Christian a leader? Yes, to the extent that we seek to influence others and make a difference in the lives around us. Are we exercising servant leadership? Yes, if we have centred ourselves in the hand of God and are leading out of a relationship with God in which we know we are '*called, loved by God and kept for Jesus Christ*', and if we are seeking to make a difference in the world by investing ourselves in relationships with those around us that are characterized by '*mercy, peace and love*'.

Principles of Servant Leadership

You are probably familiar with the powerful words of Ezekiel to the leaders of Israel in Ezekiel 34. If these are not immediately familiar, I encourage you to reread them regularly. In a scathing denunciation of leaders who used their power and position to get fat off God's flock rather than shepherd them, Ezekiel reminds us all of our accountability to God for the exercise of our leadership. It is a strong message, but it strikes a note of accountability to God that anyone engaging in the leadership of others should keep in mind.

That is precisely the image that sits in Jude's mind as he writes against some would-be leaders in his community. Six hundred years after Ezekiel, nothing has changed. Jude, the brother of our Lord, challenges the self-proclaimed leaders for the same misuse of power that God had addressed through Ezekiel. Jude uses the language of Ezekiel as he addresses his community of believers, counselling them against the leadership of false teachers within their ranks who are flaunting their power and seeking to promote themselves as the leaders of this Christian community.

In his powerful critique of their leadership, Jude uses five graphic images of the non-leader, and in so doing, I believe, gives us five working principles for effective servant leadership.

Principle 1: Leadership is about influence and service

Jude's first image is of 'shepherds who feed only themselves'. These leaders use their power for their own benefit. As we see in Ezekiel and elsewhere, the shepherd is a common image for leadership in the Bible, modelling the care and investment that the leader must make for the growth and nurture of the followers. Jude, however, confronts the false leaders in the community to which he writes for precisely the same error that Ezekiel attacked. They are using their power, not for the nurture of the community, but to draw people to themselves, to put themselves on a pedestal above the rules and values of the community. They are getting fat off the flock.

Servant leadership, on the other hand, is community-directed. It uses its power for the growth of those who are being led and the accomplishment of the shared mission of the community.

In its broadest definition, leadership is a relationship of influence. It is a relationship between two people in which one person seeks to influence the vision, values, attitudes or behaviours of the other. This definition makes it clear that everyone exercises leadership. At one time or another, we all seek to exert such influence and thus engage in leadership, at least if anyone is influenced!

When leadership is formally granted to a person by a group, community or organization – when that person is given the responsibility of being a shepherd – that leadership carries with it the expectation that the influence will be directed towards two purposes: the accomplishment of a mission or objective shared by the leader and the followers and the care and nurture of the community or organization.

Personally, leadership is a relationship of influence. Organizationally, it is a relationship of influence with purpose: maintaining the community and achieving the shared mission. When leadership is truly exercised in our organizations and in our churches, the mission is being accomplished and people are growing into community.

Principle 2: Leadership is about vision and hope

Jude's second image is just as potent. Non-servant leaders are 'clouds without rain, blown along by the wind'. Imagine a farmer in a hot desert countryside trying to scratch out a living in the harsh climate. As he looks to the sky, he sees clouds heading his way. The promise of rain looms large on the horizon. He has a vision of crops growing, of food on the table. And yet the clouds pass by, blown on the wind, failing to deliver on their promise. The vision withers. Another powerful image. Jude is accusing the false leaders of promising a future to the people, but not delivering. They are too intent on following their own desires and pursuing their spiritual visions to empower the dreams of the people they claim to lead.

Leadership is about vision. It is about tomorrow, about hope, about mission. Leadership articulates a compelling vision for tomorrow that captures the imagination of the followers and energizes their attitudes and actions in the present. It gives meaning and value to living. Leadership in community focuses the dreams and commitments of the people on a shared vision of the mission that brings them together, and then leadership works with the people to see that that mission is accomplished. Leadership is a relationship of influence that points people to a shared vision that shapes their living today in such a way that the vision is realized.

Servant leadership offers hope, it offers vision and it delivers on its promise. Servant leadership empowers people. It makes a difference.

Principle 3: Leadership is about character and trust

The third image is of 'autumn trees without fruit, uprooted – twice dead'. Trees without roots produce no fruit. This image, too, focuses on the expectation of results. The leadership of the false teachers did not produce growth. There was no fruit, no product to show for the leadership that was being exercised. And Jude is not surprised since the leadership of these 'non-leaders' is not rooted in the love of God for his people. They are doubly useless – not grounded in a relationship empowered by God and therefore not producing any growth in their community.

As Jude recognized in his opening verses, leadership arises from character. Recent research has shown a direct link between leadership and credibility. Leadership is a relationship of trust. We listen to people we trust. We accept the influence of a person whose character we respect. Leadership is grounded in the faith, beliefs, commitments and values of the leader. Leadership that produces fruit is rooted in the character of the leader. It is impossible to provide consistent leadership out of insecurity. Leadership emerges from secure people, from men and women who know who they are and live authentically in the security of that knowledge. The person who lives securely in the knowledge of the love of God will be a person whose influence is sought, whose leadership produces fruit.

What is the fruit of effective leadership? Warren Bennis, the distinguished professor of leadership at the University of Southern California, says that the three things people want from leaders are direction, trust and hope. Leadership points people in the right direction, showing them how what they are doing contributes to the shared mission of the community. Leadership believes in people and fosters relationships of trust between members of the community. It points people to God and roots their identity, dignity and security in their relationship with God in Christ. And leadership offers hope. It provides a vision that lifts the eyes of the follower up from the path they are walking to the horizon of God's eternal perspective and reminds them why they have life – to enjoy a relationship with God!

Principle 4: Leadership is about relationships and power

The fourth picture in Jude's description of these leaders describes them as 'wild waves of the sea, foaming up their shame'. Jude focuses on the power in the waves of the sea and leaves us with the feeling of unbounded power, power without purpose, leaving a trail of debris behind it. The self-appointed leaders in the community were using their influence to make a big splash, but they were not going anywhere. They were not working for the mission or unity of the community or the development of the people, but were divisive and contentious, flaunting a lifestyle that denied the lordship of Christ.

Leadership is a relationship of power. It is the exercise of power. Power is the potential for influence. It denotes the character or resources that others see in you that cause them to accept your influence. It may be the authority of your position. It may be the spirituality of your character. It may be the benefits you can provide (or the harm you can do). It may be the knowledge or skills that you possess. Power is at the heart of leadership, but power exists only when someone sees in you a reason to accept your influence. At that moment you exercise power and have the opportunity to lead. But power needs purpose. Power without purpose leaves a wake of debris, a trail of litter. Tornadoes have power, but look what they do. Power needs to be leashed to purpose. The power that permits leadership in communities must be directed to the mission that forms the community. Leadership must be responsible and accountable. Leadership is a relationship of influence with a purpose. Servant leadership points people away from the leader to the mission of the community and empowers their individual contribution towards that mission.

Principle 5: Leadership is about dependency and accountability

This fifth image offers another timely corrective to false leadership, describing such leaders as 'wandering stars, for whom blackest darkness has been reserved forever'. These leaders are like shooting stars, streaking onto the scene with flash and excitement but eventually fading and disappearing. There are short-term gains but no long-term perseverance. Such leadership that may offer a quick fix but does not nurture the long-range health of the community. There is a lot of activity, but no relationship.

Leadership is about people. It is about relationship. Leadership is a relationship of influence with a purpose; the achievement of the shared mission and the nurture of the community. Leaders are dependent upon the people. They are not charismatic comets racing alone across the sky. Leadership is a relationship of dependency. Leaders need followers. They are dependent upon the community because, in the end, leadership is in the hands of followers. It exists only when someone decides to follow, decides to accept the influence. Max DePree, the author of the best-selling *Leadership is an Art*, says that one of the responsibilities of a leader is to say thanks[17] – an acknowledgement of dependence. In the final analysis, it is always the one who follows who determines if leadership is being exercised. It does not matter how much power or charisma you think you possess, how exciting you think your vision is. What matters is, does someone choose to accept your influence and alter his or her vision, values, attitudes or behaviours.[18] Leadership is a relationship of influence with a purpose, perceived by those who choose to follow.

So what?

So what? What does this mean for you? What will you do with your power? Will you lead to empower others or will you use your power for your own benefit – to gain recognition and solidify your position and status?

Sometimes you may not think you have much power, or you may think that you exercise little leadership. Remember, however, that if leadership is a relationship of influence and power, the potential for leadership is what others see in you. It is the strength, gifts and resources that other people see in you that gives you the opportunity to lead – to influence their beliefs, their values, their behaviours. Knowledge is power; information is power; personal integrity and confidence of vision are perceived as power. The security you have in your own relationship with God gives you a spiritual power that can impact the lives of those around you.

Will you be a servant leader? Will you make a difference in the lives of those around you? Whether you are in a formal position of leadership or simply engage others in relationships, you already are equipped to lead. Out of your biblical knowledge, your maturing relationship with God in Christ, your integrated Christian worldview, you can make a difference in the world. Your decision is what you will do with this power. Will you use your education, your resources, your spiritual maturity for your own benefit, to feed yourself, or will you use your power for the growth and nurture of people? Will you empower others? Will you be caring, encouraging and motivating? Will you acknowledge your accountability to God? Will you offer vision and deliver what you promise? Will you make a difference in this world?

God has given you gifts and abilities. You are increasing your knowledge and skills. This gives you the power to influence others, to make a difference in the lives of the people around you. You are a shepherd. And the prophets are waiting to pass judgement. How will you use the power that God has entrusted to you? That is a sobering question. And if it were all that Jude had to say we would be left with only an awesome challenge of what it means to be a servant leader and a sense of anxiety in the face of divine accountability. But Jude does not stop here. He goes on to remind us of the continuing sources of power available to the servant leader who wants to make a difference.

Power for the Servant Leader

> But, dear friends, remember what the apostles of our Lord Jesus Christ foretold. They said to you, 'In the last times, there will be scoffers who will follow their own ungodly desires.'

These are the people who divide you, who follow mere natural instincts and do not have the Spirit.

But you, dear friends, build yourselves up in your most holy faith, and pray in the Holy Spirit. Keep yourselves in God's love as you wait for the mercy of our Lord Jesus Christ to bring you to eternal life.

Be merciful to those who doubt; snatch others from the fire and save them; to others show mercy mixed with fear – hating even the clothing stained by corrupted flesh.

To him who is able to keep you from falling and to present you before his glorious presence without fault and with great joy – to the only God our Saviour be glory, majesty, power and authority, through Jesus Christ our Lord, before all ages, now and forevermore! Amen. (Jude 17–25)

Where do we get this power to be servants who lead, to be shepherds who feed and nurture the flocks? Jude concludes his letter to Christian leaders by reminding them of four sources of power available to the servant leader today:

- **The content of God's Word.** Servant leaders are instructed to 'build yourselves up in your most holy faith', that is, to be grounded in the content of the Word of God – the body of truth handed down to us by the prophets and apostles, the Scriptures of the Old and New Testaments. Knowledge is power, and we have the Word of God that we might know God. Equipped with that knowledge, we have something to say to this world.
- **The communion of the Spirit.** The servant leader is to 'pray in the Holy Spirit'. In other words, he or she is to live in the presence and the power of God in Christ through the Spirit of God. In prayer, prompted by and empowered by the Spirit of Christ, we have access directly to God – the source of all glory, power and authority. It is in prayer that we find the wisdom of God – that we are able to see things from God's perspective. In prayer we centre ourselves in the hand of God, and out of the identity and security of God's hand we have power to engage others in relationships of influence.

- **A covenant in Christ.** Jude reminds us of our covenantal relationship with God in Christ when he tells us to 'keep yourselves in God's love as you wait for the mercy of our Lord Jesus Christ to bring you to eternal life'. For our part we are expected to 'keep ourselves in God's love', which Jesus has taught us means to obey his commandments (Jn. 15:10). The servant leader is obedient, seeking to live a life worthy of our God. If that were the end of the sentence, this would be a poor source of power. But Jude goes on to remind us also of God's part in this covenantal relationship. God expects obedience; he offers mercy – mercy leading to eternal life. Remember, mercy is that covenantal commitment to maintain our end of the agreement even when the other person fails. The servant leader is one who trusts in the mercy of God – who knows that God reaches out in Christ to provide the very obedience that we cannot live up to ourselves. It is this covenantal commitment by God that gives us the confidence to be servant leaders. Otherwise the task would be impossible.

- **A calling to commitment.** The servant leader who has experienced God's covenant faithfulness – God's gracious forgiveness – is called to '*be merciful*', a keeper of commitments in all leadership relationships. Servant leadership means committing ourselves to be there in another's future as a friend, as one who cares, regardless of the circumstances that occur between now and then, regardless of the path our organizational roles may lead us. It means committing ourselves to the relationship even when the other person follows a path that we cannot walk.

  Jude calls the Christian leader to commit to those who are in doubt about the direction of their lives; to confront those who have chosen to follow false leaders in a relationship of loving commitment. But even if they do not respond, he calls servant leaders to continue to commit themselves to the relationship even as they stand against the beliefs and behaviours of their friend. Servant leaders are called to make commitments in relationships to others – caring commitments that earn one the right to be heard, the right to influence. Leaders who care can make a difference in this world.

Four sources of power for the servant leader; power with which to influence others, to make a difference in this world for God. We are servants called to exercise leadership wherever God has placed us; shepherds who have been given power to feed. The prophets are waiting to pass judgement. What will you do with your power?

Jude knows that alone we cannot do much. But with God we can be leaders of influence. Servants who make a difference. It is to the God who holds on to us that we point people when we seek to exercise leadership as Christians. As Jude says, ending his letter with the well-known benediction:

To him who is able to keep you from falling and to present you before his glorious presence without fault and with great joy – to the only God, our Saviour be glory, majesty, power and authority, through Jesus Christ our Lord, before all ages, now and forevermore! (Jude 25)

Notes

[1] Robert Greenleaf, formerly an executive with AT&T, was the first to apply the concept of leadership as serving to the business world in his book *Servant Leadership* (New York: Paulist Press, 1977).
[2] Margaret Craven, *I Heard the Owl Call My Name* (New York: Dell Publishing, 1973).
[3] Paul Hersey and Kenneth H. Blanchard, *Management of Organizational Behavior* (Englewood Cliffs, N.J.: Prentice Hall, 1988[5]), 5.
[4] Howard Gardner, *Leading Minds* (New York: Basic Books, 1996), 8.
[5] James MacGregor Burns, *Leadership* (New York: Harper & Row, 1978).
[6] Tom Peters and Nancy Austin, *A Passion for Excellence* (New York: Warner Books, 1989), 354–359.
[7] Peter Koestenbaum, *The Heart of Business* (Dallas: Saybrook Publishing Company, 1987), 352.

[8] James M. Kouzes and Barry Z. Posner, *Credibility* (San Francisco: Jossey-Bass, 1993), 22.

[9] Koestenbaum, *Heart*, 354–355.

[10] Parker J. Palmer, 'Leading from Within', *Insights on Leadership* (New York: John Wiley, 1998), 205.

[11] Os Guinness, *The Call* (Nashville: Word Publishing, 1998), 4.

[12] Henri Nouwen, *In the Name of Jesus* (New York: Crossroad, 1989), 28.

[13] Nouwen, *Name*, p. 31.

[14] Mary C. Richards, *Centering in Pottery, Poetry and the Person* (Middletown, Conn.: Wesleyan University Press, 1964), in Charlotte F. Speight, *Hands in Clay* (Sherman Oaks, Calif.: Alfred Publishing, 1979), 217.

[15] Henri Nouwen, *Reaching Out: The Three Movements of the Spiritual Life* (Garden City, N.Y.: Image Books, 1986), 48.

[16] Jude 18–19.

[17] Max DePree, *Leadership is an Art* (East Lansing: Michigan State University Press, 1987), 11.

[18] H. Gardner, *Minds*, 38, notes that even the Stalins and Saddams of the world have to persuade even as they invoke instruments of terror to control their followers.

Chapter II

The Servant Leader

Jude provides us with an outline for approaching the topic of relational leadership – five biblical principles drawn from the struggles of his own Christian community. Each chapter in this study will explore one of these principles and apply it to the contemporary context of leadership and organizations.

These principles and the struggles they address are not unique to Jude's community. They speak to the core of the leadership relationship in every community of people that seeks to organize itself around a vision or purpose. The biblical narrative is filled with stories of men and women and communities attempting to work out an effective model of relational leadership. My favourite biblical drama is the story of the Colossian church as we see it in Paul's letters to the Colossians and to Philemon – a real-life community of men and women struggling with issues of leadership, relationship, diversity and conflict. The story of the Colossian church is the story of human organizations. And each player in this drama has something to teach us about relational leadership and organizational community. As we move from the context of Jude's situation to leadership in the 21st century, I would like to locate each leadership principle in the real-life narrative of Colosse. The leaders, servants and community there present a model for relational leadership that defines what it means to be leaders who serve. In the story of Onesimus, Philemon, Tychicus and Paul, there is a place for each of us.

Shepherds: Servants Assigned to Care for the Sheep

In the first chapter, I set the theme for this study by looking at Jude, the half-brother of Jesus, as he criticizes some would-be leaders in his Christian community. His little letter offers us two contrasting pictures of a Christian leader. On the one hand, we see Jude, humbly pointing away from himself, describing himself as a servant, rather than claiming his legitimate status as a brother of the Lord. On the other hand, we see the active and visible leaders of the community using their roles for their own benefit, growing fat off the flock. *Shepherds who feed only themselves.*

In those biting words, in the contrasts posed by this letter, we see the biblical model of leadership. Shepherds are there for the sheep! Shepherds by definition are servants entrusted with the care of the flock. It is a position of responsibility and service, not status and power. The sheep do not exist for the shepherd. The shepherd was hired because of the sheep.

> Leadership is about service, about shepherds who care for the sheep.

Onesimus: Leader as Servant

Enter the narrative of the Colossian church. Step into the sandals of Onesimus. How would you feel? You finally got away from the work that was grinding you down, burning you out. Perhaps you did leave with some uncomfortable circumstances, but you took the step! You left to find yourself, to figure out what you are going to do with your life. Away from your home, far from the responsibility of your work, you have time to do some thinking. And some of that thinking may be life changing!

In relationship with new friends, you begin to put the pieces of your life together. In the context of a new community, you meet the resurrected Christ and begin to think through the implications of his claim upon your life.

A place like this, away from the pressures and responsibilities of your normal life, is a gift from God; a privilege to be enjoyed and cherished. It is an opportunity to grow and to be changed. You feel like a different person in this supportive community with these encouraging friends.

But now you have to go back. Back to your community, back perhaps to uncomfortable circumstances, to old responsibilities and liabilities. You go back a new person, or at least a renewed person. What does it feel like to leave this supportive community that nurtures your new growth and development, to go back to the people you left behind?

That's the position that Onesimus found himself in. Onesimus left his life in Colosse, where he had been a slave on the staff of Philemon, a well-known leader in the Colossian church. Illegally he had run off, betraying his relationship of trust and, probably to finance his trip, he stole from his master before he went.

Somehow, in his flight he ended up with the apostle Paul. We do not know the circumstances of how they met or how Paul ended up converting Onesimus so that he became a follower of Christ. But we do know that a strong relationship developed between Onesimus and his new friend. He stayed with Paul, learned from him, cared for him and was loved by Paul in return. A close bond was formed between the two. But somewhere in his education, somewhere in the discipling process, Paul and Onesimus agreed that it was time for him to return to Colosse – to go back to his community, return to his position as a slave to Philemon, restore the broken relationships and learn to serve God and grow within that community.

Paul writes a letter to Philemon to pave the way for Onesimus' return, building strongly on his personal relationships with Philemon and Onesimus. He also writes a letter to the Colossian church to encourage them since they will be the context of Christian community in which the reconciliation of one of their elders and his newly converted runaway slave must take place.

Paul then gives both letters and Onesimus to another friend and colleague, Tychicus, and sends him off to Colosse to make this all work – to show that Christian faith can be integrated into the fabric of life and work and relationships;

that Christian community can deal with conflict and forgiveness and new beginnings. Paul hopes to encourage Philemon, Onesimus and the Colossians to listen to and learn from each other as they work out how their common faith will lead them through their damaged relationships and pain.

Three things strike me about Onesimus' return to Colosse: He is stepping out of his comfort zone; he has a friend to encourage him; and he is going back to serve.

Stepping out of the comfort zone

It must have been a painful experience for Onesimus to leave Paul and return to Colosse. Not only was he leaving the man who had introduced him to Jesus, he was leaving a friend and a community of encouragement – a network of supportive relationships. He was leaving a place where he could grow, a place where he was loved, a place that valued him and his contributions, a place where his personal spiritual pilgrimage was understood. Onesimus was leaving the safety of a community that had shared his experience and nurtured his growth to go to one that was predisposed to receive him with hostility. He was leaving the comfort and security of the known to risk the unknown future.

Yet Paul and Onesimus agree that he must leave the comfort of the community and return if he is to grow personally and make a difference in the lives of the people in Colosse. Leadership is about leaving your comfort zone and taking a risk to engage those around you.

The tradition of the early church frequently equates the Onesimus of our story with the later Bishop Onesimus of Ephesus. This cannot be proved. But if it is true, the runaway slave from Colosse learned well from his mentors and became one who was regarded as a leader and teacher in the church. From a slave of Philemon, mentored by Paul, Onesimus may have become the Bishop of Ephesus, leading the leaders of the church.

Taking friends with you

The second thing I see in the Onesimus story is the importance of encouraging relationships. Paul did not send

Onesimus back to Colosse alone. He sent him with a friend
– Tychicus.

Tychicus is the least known player in this Colossian drama.
He is a friend and colleague of Paul who was with Onesimus
during his conversion and growth. He knows Onesimus well,
and we can assume that he has become an important friend
to the converted slave.

When Paul sends Onesimus back to Colosse, he surely
sends him out in the power of God. But he also sends with
him a friend to support and encourage him as he returns to
his home. Tychicus is there to encourage Onesimus as he
faces Philemon, to confront Onesimus if fear makes him
falter, to pave the way for him with Philemon and the Colossian church and to pray for him and give advice as needed.

Again, the story has parallels for today. Whether taking up
new responsibilities of leadership or continuing in service,
we all need mentors and friends to guide and inspire, to challenge and support us as we live and work. All of us need a
Tychicus around to encourage us and hold us accountable to
our growth and our calling. If you do not have such a relationship in your work setting, I encourage you to find such
relationships and commit to one another to keep in touch
and provide the caring encouragement, the listening ear and
the loving accountability that we all need. Leadership is risky
business. It takes more from the servant leader than it gives.
We need one another.

A few years ago a very competent leader accepted the position of president at a Canadian theological school. Within six
months he had encountered enough problems to drive him to
despair. During Easter week he had a major conflict with his
faculty and board. With no one to encourage him and hold
him up before God, he walked back to his office and killed
himself. That is extreme. It is tragic. It is hard to understand,
but it underlines the vulnerability of leadership as we leave
our security and comfort and go out to serve. We need to
hold one another up before God and engage in encouraging
relationships. Stop and think about it now: Who is your
Tychicus? Who stands with you as you exercise your leadership responsibilities?

Going back to serve

The third thing we can learn from Onesimus may be the most important. He is going back to serve. In our familiarity with Bible stories, we look at what God has accomplished in his grace and often forget the feelings or anxieties of the person. We hear about Onesimus the bishop and assume that God is sending Onesimus back to Colosse to become a bishop. Maybe this is true, but Onesimus does not know it! Paul is only asking Philemon to receive him as a brother *and* reinstate him as his slave. Onesimus is going back to serve. He does not go back a free man. He goes back as Philemon's servant. The very act of returning to Colosse was an acknowledgement of this status and a willingness to serve. Maybe Onesimus did become a bishop. But he did not go back to Colosse to be a bishop and do something great for God. He returned to be a servant.

Herman Hesse, in his novel *The Journey to the East*, describes a quest to discover the high council of a secret order in the East. The main characters are seeking to meet the leader of this society and be introduced to the fundamental truth of life. Throughout their journey they are guided and assisted by a servant assigned to care for them, carry their luggage and ease their passage. At the end of the journey, they finally arrive at the grand throne room of the society and who should walk out in the golden robes of the league president, but their servant.[1] Onesimus returned to Colosse after a time of instruction and growth with Paul and his friends. He left comfort behind, and returned to Colosse with a friend to take his position as a slave to Philemon and a servant to his new master, Jesus Christ. That is the calling of the Christian leader! We are called to be servants of Jesus Christ who care for the people who have been entrusted to us and point them to God in every act of leadership and service that we undertake. Leadership is a relationship of service – a relationship in which influence and leadership flow from service, not from position or status.

Leadership: A Relationship of Influence

What is this thing called leadership? The leadership model that I work from has become popular over the last two decades. Researchers, consultants, corporate and non-profit executives have observed a transition in leadership models evolving in the West in recent years. This 'new paradigm', as it is often labelled, reached popular acceptance with the publication of *In Search of Excellence*, in 1982.[2] Tom Peters and Robert Waterman were the first to put the new research findings in a popular form that captured the attention of leaders, particularly in North America. Since the appearance of their book on the management best-seller lists, a steady stream of publications have continued to present a model of leadership that is relational, vision-driven and value-shaped. Peter Drucker, Peter Block, Warren Bennis, Max DePree, Tom Peters, Steven Covey, James O'Toole, Charles Handy, Peter Senge and many other names have become familiar to the readers of the leadership literature.

While many of these writers are committed Christians and support a relational approach to leadership because of its recognizable grounding in biblical values, the model has emerged primarily because it works. It treats people with dignity, offers hope and gives meaning, but the bottom line for most organizations is that it has proven effective in addressing the organization's mission. I want to look at a pragmatic model for leadership that I believe is founded on strong biblical principles.

We need to remember that we are talking about a model for leadership – a proven model – but not necessarily one that can be found consistently lived in many organizations. It sets out the principles against which we can measure our leadership and against which we see our shortcomings. I am trying to live out at Regent College everything I talk about here, but those who have been to Regent know that we experience all of the struggles of any human community. But before God we keep trying.

I should also underline here that I am writing out of my experience and reading which have been heavily centred in

North America. Since moving to Canada in 1988, I have observed subtle but distinct differences between Canadian and American attitudes towards leadership. I do not pretend to know much about the cultural assumptions and structures that shape leadership in other parts of the world. If you work in a different cultural setting, or even if you serve within a particular ethnic subculture within North America, please remember that, like most writers, I see things from a particular perspective, and you will need to work with me to translate these ideas into the appropriate context for your setting. However, I do want to explore some guiding principles for leadership that I believe are both effective and biblical.

So, what is leadership? What is leadership all about? What is a leader? In this and the next chapter on vision, I will focus primarily on the leader. In the remaining three chapters, I will try to be a little more practical and look at strategies for serving as a leader.

People have been defining leadership for years. The variety of technical and anecdotal definitions is extensive and often more confusing than clarifying. Gary Yukl, in *Leadership in Organizations*, defines leadership as 'the influence process whereby intentional influence is exerted by the leader over followers.[3] Paul Hersey and Kenneth Blanchard, in their classic text *Management of Organizational Behavior*, see leadership as a broader concept than management. If management is working with and through individuals and groups to accomplish organizational goals, 'leadership occurs any time one attempts to influence the behavior of an individual or group, regardless of the reason'.[4]

> Leadership is a relationship of influence.

Leadership is a relationship

Leadership is first and foremost a relationship between two people. Even in a group or organizational setting where we may be responsible for leading a number of people, we are still leading in the context of specific relationships. Leader and follower or, as John Gardner the author of *On Leader-*

ship likes to say, leader and constituent – two people engaged in a relationship.[5] That is the specific context of leadership.

Leadership is influence

In the definitions to which I just referred, leadership is defined as the process of one person influencing another. It is a relationship of influence in which the leader seeks to influence the behaviour, attitudes, vision, values or beliefs of another. It is an intentional relationship with a purpose – a relationship of influence.

In his taxonomy of leadership research, Gary Yukl identifies eleven different forms of influence used by leaders today.[6] Knowing the specific types is not nearly as important as recognizing that we lead or influence others in a variety of ways. Leadership is more than telling someone to do something. In fact, research has shown that leaders who seek to lead primarily with the first three types of influence described below may be quite effective when they are physically present, but they lose their ability to influence and lead the follower when they are not present.

Yukl's influence types can be described as follows:

➤ **Legitimate request**
  The leader is directive and requests that the follower do a particular thing. The follower recognizes the authority or 'right' of the leader to make the request and responds accordingly.

  Example: *An executive asks a secretary to type a letter and the influence is accepted. The letter is typed because both know that is why the secretary was hired and the request is legitimate.*

➤ **Instrumental compliance**
  The follower believes that the action requested by the leader will provide a specific desirable outcome promised by the leader. The leader in this case is still directive but needs to convince the follower to act and has the ability to reward the carrying out of his/her wishes.

Example: *If my students turn in a paper for my class they can receive credit for the course.*

➤ **Coercion**
Here the follower acts to avoid adverse outcomes implied in a failure to act. The leader again needs to convince the follower to act and possesses the ability to punish the follower for not complying.

Example: *Failure to turn in the paper will result in a failing grade for the course.*

➤ **Rational faith**
The follower acts because he or she has faith in the expertise or credibility of the leader. The leader is believed to have the knowledge or competence to be followed. This type of influence may be a directive request, a consultative dialogue or simply the offering of advice.

Example: *The church board will listen to the pastor on worship issues because he or she has been trained in spiritual leadership and worship.*

➤ **Rational persuasion**
The follower is convinced that the action desired by the leader is the best way for the follower to meet his or her own objectives. In this case the followers are persuaded that the actions requested by the leader are right and appropriate and will help them accomplish their own personal goals. With this type of influence, the leader moves away from directive leadership and moves into consultative dialogue, seeking to persuade the follower that this is a good thing to do.

Example: *Kevin agreed to take on a research project for the trustees because he could use it for his doctoral dissertation.*

➤ **Inspirational appeal**
In this type of influence the followers respond because it makes them feel good and supports their values. The

leader is making an appeal to the values of the follower. This model is regularly used in preaching. Like the apostle Paul, the pastor appeals to the congregation to live up to their calling and seeks to influence them to live out their Christian life more fully. Again, this is not directive leadership; it is more consultation or coaching leadership.

Example: *The pastor urges a member to visit a parishioner in the hospital as a Christian service to the congregation.*

➢ **Indoctrination**
Here Yukl talks about a situation in which the follower internalizes values or beliefs that will cause the action to happen as natural behaviour. This type of influence is almost completely non-directive. There may not even be a visible link between the efforts of the leader to pass on values and beliefs and the response of the follower acting out of those values. And yet it may be one of the most powerful forms of influence that we use as Christian leaders.

Example: *In many ways, while we might not like the label, this is what we are about in Sunday School, confirmation, preaching and the teaching of theology. We are seeking to embed a set of values and beliefs that will cause Christlike behaviour to emerge naturally throughout a person's life.*

➢ **Information distortion**
Another uncomfortable label, but a frequently used influence type. Here the follower receives only those data that will stimulate the desired action. The rest is screened out by the leader. When information is selectively given, it can produce a desired action. When we offer only one recommendation to our people and limit them to one choice, they will probably choose what we recommend.

Example: *Telling you the office lock does not work and someone entered the church and took a purse will get one response. Telling you the purse was taken by one of the pre-schoolers in the church because there is not enough supervision will provoke a different response – even if both are true. That is what Yukl calls information distortion. And we use this type more often then we are probably comfortable admitting.*

> ## Situational engineering
Here the leader changes the follower's situation to make a particular action more advantageous.

Example: *The placement of desks in an office will facilitate or discourage conversations. Passing the offering plate down the aisle on Sunday morning is more conducive to increasing the offering than letting people stop by the treasurer's office on the way out.*

> ## Personal identification
This type is similar to rational faith. Here the follower copies the actions or behaviour of someone who is respected and admired. This relationship is what mentoring is about when formally acknowledged. But note that this kind of influence is going on all the time whether we know it or not. People watch leaders and learn. Our actions and behaviours teach as much about our beliefs and values as our words. People who admire leaders will copy their behaviours and be influenced by them without the leader necessarily knowing.

Research has shown that this type of influence, this building of personal relationships often called *referential power*, is the most effective leadership when the leader is not with the follower. It is leadership that lasts. I often tell the faculty at Regent College that they teach as much by what they do between classes as by what they teach in class. People watch people they like and are influenced by their behaviours. Leaders are models.

Example: *One day as I was buying a cup of coffee at Regent's coffee bar, I overheard a student in line behind me commenting to another student, 'Look, the President is paying for his coffee.' I am not sure what kind of concept of leaders they had that would cause them to think otherwise, but the point driven home again for me was the fact that people are watching ... even watching little things like whether you pay for coffee like they do or expect special treatment because you are leader.*

➤ **Decision identification**
This one also is important in relational leadership. When people are involved in the planning and decision process, when they feel like part of a team, they take ownership of the action. Participative management, team building and letting people share in decisions that will impact their lives and work creates an ownership of outcomes that greatly facilitates appropriate actions. With this style of influence we have moved completely away from directive leadership into the realm of participation and delegation.

Now, why bother with defining influence types? Again, let me repeat that knowing these eleven types is not what is important. What is important is recognizing that leadership is much more than giving direction. We influence in relationship. We influence by our decisions and our actions. *Leadership is a relationship of influence.*

Leadership is perceived by the followers

This is an important principle that is often overlooked. I am regularly surprised by leaders who assume that they are leaders because of their position or because they want to be. David Hubbard, the former President of Fuller Seminary and a friend and mentor of mine, liked to tell the story of his little grandson Jeffrey. Once when David and Ruth were walking in the park with Jeffrey, they began to stroll off in one direction while Jeffrey was still playing. Seeing them leaving, Jeffrey came running up, his chubby little legs churning, calling out, 'Wait for me, I'm the leader!' Having the title of leader does not mean you are providing leadership. We can exert every one of the influence types we have just reviewed, but unless someone *chooses* to accept that influence, we have not led. It is very important that those of us in leadership always remember that our followers have choice, and that our leadership is always dependent upon their choosing to follow.

Leadership style is adapted to the follower's maturity

Leaders are dependent upon followers who choose to accept their influence. This dependency of the leader upon followers is what makes the leadership relationship so important. Leaders must adjust their attempts to influence and shape their leadership to the follower they want to influence. Paul Hersey and Kenneth Blanchard have developed a leadership model that sees leadership as a relational continuum with four distinct styles of leadership behaviour tied directly to the specific follower. Their classic text *Management of Organizational Behavior* describes this model, often called contingency leadership or situational leadership.[7]

The model has two axes, representing two continua. One relates to the amount of task-directive behaviour the leader uses and the other measures the amount of relational support the leader provides. Task-directive behaviour ranges from telling someone exactly what to do to full delegation in which the person makes his or her own choices. Relational-support behaviour ranges from standing alongside someone, holding their hand and encouraging them, to standing back and trusting them to do it without you. When these continua are plotted on horizontal and vertical axes, the model makes it possible to identify four quadrants or leadership styles. These Hersey and Blanchard label telling, selling, participating and delegating.

A *telling* style of leadership is highly task directive with little relational encouragement. The *selling* style remains fairly directive but engages in much more relational support behaviour. The *participating* style is much less directive but

Situational Leadership®

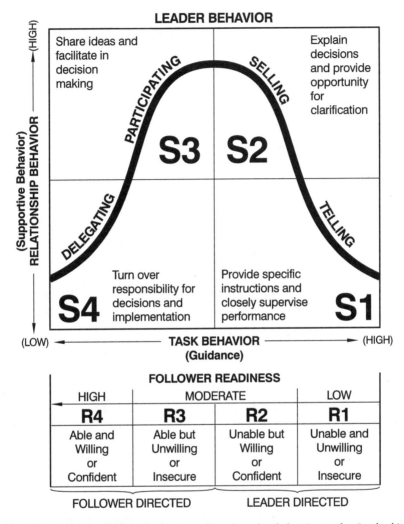

Note: Situational Leadership® is a registered trademark of the Center for Leadership Studies, Inc. All rights reserved. Reprinted with permission.

retains a high level of relational support. Finally, the *delegating style* is quite non-directive and provides minimal relational support, trusting the follower to run with the task.

The most important element in this model, however, is not the four leadership styles themselves but the direct relationship between leadership style and the maturity of the follower. Hersey and Blanchard identify four levels of maturity in followers. At the lowest level, the followers do not know how to do the task and lack confidence in their ability to do it so they are not willing to accept responsibility for the task. When followers are low in competence and in confidence, the model suggests that the most effective leadership style will be telling: directive explanation of what needs to be done with little relational encouragement that would only reinforce their unwillingness to take responsibility.

At the next level of maturity, the followers still do not know how to do the task but they are willing to learn and want to accept responsibility for the assignment. Hersey and Blanchard call for a selling or consultative style of leadership when the followers are low in competence but high in confidence. Here the leader remains directive, telling the followers what they need to know to do the job, but engages them relationally to reinforce their willingness to accept responsibility.

At the third level of maturity, the followers basically know how to do the job but lack confidence in their ability to do it alone. Contingency leadership adapts to a participating style that becomes non-directive but participates in a close relationship, encouraging and believing in the person to bolster confidence.

The highest level of maturity assumes that the followers know how to do the work and are willing to accept responsibility to see that it is done. The best style of leadership now, say Hersey and Blanchard, is delegating. There is no need to be directive since they know how to do the job and hanging around in close relationship only creates a dependence upon the leader. We need to get out of their way and trust them to lead out in getting the work done. The leader steps into the background, but is available when the follower seeks assistance.

This is only a model – a representation of two competing responsibilities of leadership: the accomplishment of the task or mission and the care and development of the followers. It is not a precise formula to resolve the complexities of human relationships! Contingency theory or situational leadership can be helpful in clarifying leadership responsibility or it can be used as an excuse for poor leadership.[8] The importance of the model is that it graphically represents several key leadership principles:

- **Leaders must adapt their leadership style to the maturity of their followers.**
  The way you choose to lead is not up to you. It is determined by the maturity level of the person you seek to influence. If leadership is exercised only when a follower chooses to follow, it behoves leaders to understand the competence and the confidence levels of those they seek to influence.

- **Followers range back and forth on the maturity continuum.**
  People do not stay at one level of maturity. A problem at home or on the way to work can reduce a person's confidence level. A change in the way things are done can reduce their competence level. A very simple example of this occurred when computers were introduced in the office. Suddenly, mature secretaries, who had been operating efficiently in quadrant four without much direct supervision, lacked competence and in many cases lost confidence as well. The leader needs to recognize these shifts and not be surprised by them. When the situation changes, the maturity level changes, and the leader needs to adapt to the appropriate relational leadership style. The secretaries needed explicit instruction in the use of computers before their competence and confidence could be brought back up to the highest level.

- **The goal of leadership is to move people up the maturity continuum.**
  The aim of leadership is to increase the competence and confidence of all of our people so that we can delegate leadership to them. This is one of the purposes of leadership. We want to grow people. We want to invest in them to move them all, if possible, to the highest levels of maturity so that they can serve as leaders in their particular areas. Success in leadership is measured by the growth of

your followers – not by how *many* followers you have, but by how much each person grows under your leadership. In Christian circles we call this process discipling.

The importance of the contingency model of leadership is the reminder that leaders must be adaptable. You must be able to change your leadership style to match the maturity level of your followers in order to grow them. Leaders who are not adaptable tend to keep followers at one static level of maturity.

Jack Balswick and I modified this model from our biblical understanding of leadership into what we called a Complementary-Empowering Model of Ministerial Leadership.[9] We reversed the task continuum and changed the labels to preaching, teaching, participating and delegating.

In addition, we added two primary elements to the situational model. First we wanted to underline what we called the *empowering curve* – adjusting the relationship between the leader and the follower to move from dependence to empowerment. This means moving decisions from the leader to the follower because, in many ways, the power to decide is also the power to lead. In the *preaching* style, the leader decides and tells the follower what to do by proclamation. The *teaching* style acknowledges the relationship. There is consultation and the leader decides only after hearing the opinions of the follower. In the *participating* style, the leader and the follower make the decision together. And in the *delegating* style, the decision is delegated to the follower to make.

The second point Jack and I wanted to make focuses on adaptability. As Hersey and Blanchard have underlined, leadership must be adaptable. Leaders must be able to range from telling to delegating in their leadership behaviour. For some that is natural, for others it is hard to learn. Some leaders simply work best in one style, with one level of follower maturity. While such leadership may be effective, it does not grow people. Drawing on the biblical concept of community and gifted members, we suggest that it may be better to have a complementary leadership team rather than expecting one

A Complementary-Empowering Model of Ministerial Leadership

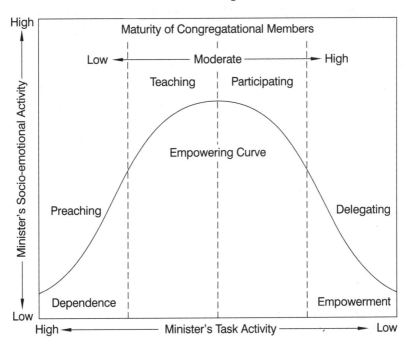

leader to work effectively with all four styles. A leadership team of clergy and laity, paid and volunteer, can ensure that someone is available with the requisite skills to provide leadership to followers as they are growing through the four stages of maturity. This reduces the burden on a single leader. In the church, a charismatic preaching pastor may need to hand members on to good interactive teachers, who in turn prepare them for coaching by disciplers who lead them to the point where they can carry out a piece of the ministry under the supervision of an organizing manager. Both Jack and I believe that leadership teams are often more effective than solo leaders. I will come back to this idea of team building later in this chapter. But before we talk about teams, let me underline a few more principles of leadership.

Leadership is a transforming relationship

James McGregor Burns in his Pulitzer Prize-winning book *Leadership* argues that there is an exchange that takes place in every leadership relationship.[10] He calls this exchange *transactional leadership*. He sees the leader and the follower exchanging something. Both gain from the influence type utilized. The followers perceive that it is to their advantage to undertake the requested action, and the leader has set up the request in order to achieve that for which he or she is responsible. Burns sees this exchange present in every leadership relationship. But he wants more. He argues that great leadership is *transforming leadership* in which the leader and the follower grow in the process. The relationship lifts both to a higher plane of maturity or morality. Burns wants the leadership relationship to accomplish more than simply making an action happen. He wants the vision, values and beliefs of the follower to be transformed and enlarged, and, in that process, he believes the leader's vision, values and beliefs will also be enriched. Transforming leadership is leadership that makes a difference in the lives of those involved beyond the task that is being completed. It lifts our eyes up from the task at hand to the horizon before us and a vision of what we can accomplish together.

Leadership is empowering

Peter Block is a management consultant who has taken Burns' vision a step further in what he calls *empowerment*. In his best-selling book *The Empowered Manager* Block calls for leadership that moves people from dependency to empowerment.[11] He wants leaders to model and encourage empowerment. For Block that means deciding on a vision for excellence in your area of responsibility and encouraging everyone else to have such a vision as well. Block, like Burns, wants leaders to see in others their potential to be more than they are today and to invest in a relationship with them that gives them the space to become everything that God intends them to become. From a Christian perspective we might add, a relationship that gives them the space to use and develop the gifts that God has given them.

Max DePree, retired Chairman of Herman Miller, Inc. and author of three best-selling books on leadership, tells a marvellous story of an empowering factory supervisor:

A young man who operated one of the machines in a Herman Miller plant had an automobile accident on the way to his girlfriend's house. He was seriously injured physically and suffered some brain damage. He obviously could no longer perform his job and when he came out of his long stay in the hospital he lived with his parents.

Several months after the accident, his supervisor was walking in downtown Grand Rapids and saw the young man, hobbling along with a walker, beside his mother. The supervisor greeted them and asked the young man why he wasn't at work.

The young man's mother was quite upset, pointing out that her son would never work again. He was permanently crippled, and would not talk anymore because of the emotional trauma. The supervisor found out that the young man was living with his parents, both of whom were retired.

The supervisor then told the young man and his mother that Herman Miller had been holding a job open for the young man and expected him to be at work the next Monday morning! And if his mother did not think he could do the job, then the supervisor expected the mother or the father to cover the job for him. And he said that he would be at their home Monday morning to pick up one of them for work!

On Monday, he was there and the young man did come in to work. Over the next weeks either he or his mother or father was there every day, filling the position and drawing the paycheque.

However, there was still the problem that he would not talk. The supervisor went to two of the women who worked in the same department as the young man and told them about the situation. They agreed to bring an extra lunch each day and eat lunch with the young man to see if they could get him to talk. Slowly he began to open up to them and then to others at the plant.

This progressed for a period of several months, until the young man was able to return to his original position as a machine operator.

Several months later, the supervisor was surprised one morning by a car honking outside his house. He went out and found the young man driving his own car, specially fitted for his handicaps and expressing deep joy and pleasure that he had his job, his income and now his own car again.[12]

This is empowering leadership – one person using his or her position in the marketplace to serve and nurture another; one person seeing in another the potential to be more than is visible today and committing him- or herself to the development of that potential.[13] *This is what servant leadership is all about.*

Servant Leadership: Strategies for Growing People

We have defined leadership as a relationship of influence – a transforming relationship in which the leader invests in the growth and development of the followers, empowering them to become what God has gifted them to be. Now, let's look at three practical applications of this empowering model for servant leadership: mentoring, coaching and team building.

Mentoring

There is a lot of talk today about mentoring and coaching. Basically this is about moving your people along the maturity development continuum – making personal investments in your followers to move them along the continuum towards leadership. Mentoring and coaching are about empowering people.

Technically speaking, *mentoring* is the more formal term, denoting an intentional, exclusive, intensive, voluntary relationship between the leader and the follower. Mentoring is a relational experience in which one person empowers another by sharing him- or herself and his or her resources. Normally, the leader and the follower agree to engage in an intentional relationship in which the leader has the follower's permission to guide him or her along a career or personal development path. This guidance occurs in an interactive learning relationship that can be initiated either by the leader or the follower.

I should underline the importance of the interactive nature of this relationship. It is what makes mentoring such a powerful teaching format. Research has shown that, while knowledge can be transmitted in a variety of forms and media, learning occurs in interactive relationships. Mentoring is an interactive learning relationship. It provides a significant point of connection in an increasingly fragmented world.

While mentoring is technically defined as a mutually intentional relationship, in some sense a form of mentoring or relational learning takes place even in relationships that are only intentional from one side. There is *passive mentoring* (what Yukl called influence by personal identification) when the follower seeks to emulate the values or behaviours of a hero or role model. The learning is happening in the follower, but the leader may be completely oblivious to the fact. *Occasional mentoring* occurs in the relationships of teachers, counsellors, tutors and sponsors. Here the teaching is usually intentional from the side of the leader, but is not always acknowledged by the followers. *Deliberate mentoring* can be seen in the relationships between parents and children, between spiritual directors and those directed, between coaches and players.

In the leadership context, when I talk about mentoring, I am talking about *an interactive learning relationship mutually recognized and defined by both leader and follower with the purpose of increasing the follower's maturity in leadership*. Such a relationship usually assumes some element of attraction. The leader sees potential in the follower worth the investment, and the follower recognizes that he or she can grow under the tutelage of the mentor and is prepared to make the investment.

I believe strongly in the value of such mentoring relationships. I have been blessed with a series of significant mentors over my life. First, there was Glenn Barker, the provost at Fuller Seminary in California, who took me on in an intentional mentoring relationship for 12 years until his death. This was very much a mentor-controlled relationship in which he deliberately set out to grow me into leadership and vulnerably opened himself up to me as a resource. He probably has shaped my life more than any other single human being.

For the past 17 years, I have been in a form of mentoring relationship with Max DePree. Max is a person whose consistent integration of faith and leadership I have always admired. He lives out of a value-shaped character that I would like to emulate. Our relationship is primarily follower-controlled. I am one of a privileged few whom Max engages in such relationships, and I have access to him for a half-day two or three times each year. These meetings are usually set up at my initiative. (Although if Max is going to be in Vancouver, he will call me and take the initiative.) I bring the agenda to each meeting and draw on his wisdom – what he is learning these days and how he would reflect on my current successes and struggles. His profound insights always send me away with a different perspective on my leadership efforts. The fact that Max finds that these are times of learning and growth for him as well always surprises me.

To a lesser extent, I had a similar relationship with David Hubbard, the former President of Fuller Seminary. I value these relationships deeply and cannot imagine trying to engage in leadership without these wise mentors to call on.

Over the years, as I have become older, and hopefully a little wiser, I have accepted relationships in which I play the mentoring role. Unless the person is on the administrative staff at Regent, the relationships usually take the follower-shaped format that I use with Max DePree. Randy, a minister, sets up meetings once or twice each year. We have been meeting now for six years. Leslie, an educator and family counsellor, set up regular meetings over a ten-year stage of her life. At the beginning we met monthly. Even now, years later, we probably talk several times each year. Doug, a minister in Alaska, flew to see me once or twice each year to test his learning. When he was a student at Regent, we met monthly, now we try to work around his trips to Vancouver. Brent is an administrator on the Regent staff. We both understand our relationship as organizationally defined and as a mentoring relationship. In that context we meet weekly in our managerial relationship and regularly over lunch to reflect on his growth in a mentoring relationship. In these times of reflection, in fact at any time, Brent has the right to ask about anything that I am doing at Regent College. In all of these relationships, I am a learner as well as a mentor. As Leslie completed her doctoral programme and Brent worked through an executive MBA programme, I had the privilege of learning from their learning as well. Sharing yourself usually teaches you something about yourself in the process. It is a good learning experience.

What about you? Can you identify intentional mentoring relationships when you think back over your life? Are you being mentored in such a relationship in your current situation? Are you engaged intentionally as a mentor now?

Mentoring is a powerful form of leadership. It is a very effective way of influencing and of being influenced, of teaching and of learning. I highly recommend that, if you are not in such a mentoring relationship, you seek out a mentor or two to learn from and with and set up some kind of accountable relationship for your own growth as a servant leader.

Coaching

Coaching is less structured than mentoring. In some ways, it is more a style of management than an individual intentional relationship. It is a way of approaching all of your leadership relationships with a servant's heart, with the mind of a player-coach. Coaching is a participative approach to leadership rather than a directive approach. It sees the leader as servant and friend, not ruler or boss. Coaches walk with their people, teaching as much by their actions as by their words. Coaching levels the hierarchical relationship of the organization and puts the leader among the people. Coaching moves people along the maturity development continuum by walking alongside them.

In the book *A Passion for Excellence* Tom Peters and Nancy Austin include a long list of characteristics that they believe describe a good coaching leader:[14]

Challenges me to do my best
Sets a good example
Never divulges a confidence
Explains the reasons for instructions and procedures
Helps me polish my thoughts before I present them to others
Is objective about things

Lets me make my own decisions
Cares about me and how I'm doing
Does not seek the limelight
Won't let me give up
Gives personal guidance and direction when I'm learning something
    new
Is empathetic and understanding
Is firm but fair
Keeps a results orientation
Makes me work out most of my own problems, but supports me
Lets me know where I stand
Listens exceptionally well
Doesn't put words in my mouth
Is easy to talk to
Keeps the promises he or she makes
Keeps me focused on the goals ahead
Works as hard or harder than anyone else
Is humble
Is proud of those managers he or she has developed
Gives credit where credit is due
Practices MBWA (Management By Walking Around)
Never says, 'I told you so'
Corrects my performance in private
Never flaunts authority
Is always straightforward
Gives at least a second chance
Maintains an open door policy
Uses language that is easy to understand
Lets bygones by bygones
Inspires loyalty
Really wants to hear my ideas, and acts on them
Lets me set my own deadlines
Celebrates successes
Is open and honest
Doesn't hide bad news
Gives me enough time to prepare for discussion
Is enthusiastic
Follows through
Is patient
Wants me to 'stretch' my skills
Gives me his or her full attention during discussions, won't be
    distracted
Has a sense of humour
Handles disagreements privately
Reassures me

Makes me feel confident
Tells me the 'whole story'
Says 'we' instead of 'I'
Makes hard work worth it
Can communicate annoyance without running wild
Is courageous
Insists on training
Is a stabilizing influence in a crisis
Gets everyone involved
Wants me to be successful
Is optimistic
Operates well under pressure, or in a rapidly changing environment
Has a reputation for competence with his or her peers
Has a good understanding of the job
Is tough and tender
Believes we can do it
Sets attainable milestones
Communicates philosophy and values
Is perceptive – doesn't require that everything be spelled out
Has a strong sense of urgency
Preserves the individuality of his or her team members
Thinks and operates at a level above that expected
Wants to make the organization the best in the industry
Is willing to act on intuition; believes feelings are facts
Empowers us
Is there when we need him or her
Enjoys his or her job
Likes to spend time with us

Coaching is a participative approach to leadership in which the leader sees him- or herself as a member of the team, working for the good of the mission, serving the community. The leader is there for the people, not the people for the leader.

Team building

Linked closely to the idea of leader as coach or servant is the idea of the followers as a team. In many ways these are two perspectives on the same relationship. Good coaches produce strong teams. How does the leadership relationship look from the perspective of the team?

Several years ago, Larry Czonka was the All-Pro fullback for the Miami Dolphins, a professional American football team. Czonka was considered the best fullback in the National Football League. About this time the World Football League was developing and offering large contracts to the great players to entice them to jump to the new league. Czonka told Don Shula, the Miami head coach, that he was considering accepting the offer. Shula told Czonka that it would be a bad idea. However, when Larry Czonka was elected All-Pro fullback again that year, he notified Shula that he was leaving Miami to join the World Football League. He said, 'I'm All Pro. I'm the best there is, and I'm worth the money.' Shula replied, 'No Larry, you are only All Pro when you have me for a coach, Bob Griese for quarterback and the Miami Dolphin team blocking for you!'

Czonka did jump to the new league and basically disappeared from the professional football scene. He was good, but his effectiveness was made possible because he was a member of a great team.[15]

John Gardner, former Secretary of Health, Education and Welfare in the United States and author of books on leadership, renewal and excellence, argues that the best leaders today form a team with the talent and skills to complement their own.[16]

Today the literature of leadership and management is focusing more and more on team approaches to leadership: coaching, participative management, work groups and task forces. The effective leader needs to be able to build and motivate a team of people who take ownership of their unit's results and participate in the decisions that affect their work experience.

I have favoured a team approach to management for years. I have tried to develop teams with 'manual' workers and with high-level 'knowledge' workers like the faculty at Regent. I am a strong believer in team leadership since I know from experience that a team has more hands than I do and more wisdom as they see things from a variety of perspectives.

After years of working with teams, I was once asked to lead a workshop on team building. To prepare for this workshop, I asked all of the members of the current team I was leading and all former members of our organization who were still in the area to join me for lunch. I would buy lunch if they would tell me what it meant to be on an effective team. I asked them to list the characteristics of a good team. I just took notes. Since that meeting I have tried to keep up with some of the research on team leadership and have found that the thirteen elements listed by my team members are supported by the literature on team building. These are the elements that people identify as important to their experience of working on a team.

1. Ownership of mission and strategies
This was a major point. They see the office as their unit. They own the goals of the unit and the way we do things. It is their operation, not just mine.

2. Shared visions and dreams
I think out loud about everything we are doing. They know where we are going and why. This transparency is important because it gives team members a chance to participate in the ideas and dreaming long before a decision is made for implementation. This participation creates the ownership they listed first. The dreams and plans become *ours*, not *mine*.

3. Communication of information
This is basically the same thing. No secrets, no surprises. Information is friendly. The more the team knows, the more it can help. I have always shared nearly all information with my staff unless it is harmful to their relationship with another person. Open communication and sharing of information develop trust. Leaders are often nervous about sharing sensitive information or information about possible plans that someone might work against. In thirty years of management, only once has a member of staff betrayed my trust and used information inappropriately. When this occurred, I simply spoke with the person and asked if that meant I could no longer share information. The person was immediately apologetic and vowed that it would not happen again, and it never has.

I do find that as president, however, sharing information can be a little more problematic. Sometimes when I think out

loud people hear 'policy', and begin to react accordingly. I
regularly have to add a preamble in conversation: 'We are
just thinking and brainstorming; this may not be the way we
should go at all.' Occasionally my openness about my
agendas and thinking does mean that people who disagree
can begin to build opposition while I am still trying to test
the idea. But I believe that is a risk worth taking. It may
create a few more headaches for leadership, but it communicates trust and it earns trust. There are some at Regent
College who may not like the direction I am leading, but
everyone knows where I am going.

4. Relaxed relationships
This may be more a matter of personal style than a requisite
for team management, but it does seem to show up on Peters'
and Austin's lists. I want to enjoy my work, and I encourage
my teams to enjoy themselves as well. I try not to take myself
or anyone else too seriously since everything I accomplish is
directly tied to their contributions. I try to encourage talking
and relaxed relationships while maintaining a professional
environment. I want people to look forward to Monday, not
to Friday! I want them to come to work on Monday eager to
see their friends and catch up on the important issues in their
lives. I believe that a team of people who like to be together
will be more productive and enjoy it.

5. Approachable leadership
The team wants to see the leader as open, available and
approachable. This often needs to be worked at. Leaders, by
virtue of the position they hold, are perceived as distant, busy
and unapproachable. An open door can help. Also I continually remind the team that they have access to me at any time.
I am there to help them get their jobs done. I must be available. I try to communicate that I am available to talk about
work or about life.

6. Trusting relationships
The relational side of the team is important. In every office I
have worked, with every team I have been part of, we have

spent a lot of time talking about life unrelated to the office operations or the organizational mission. Some years it seemed like we hired only newly-weds, and I felt like a marriage counsellor much of the time. When people trust you to be their leader, even in the limited arena of their work, they are trusting you with a part of their lives. The work relationship is strengthened if a relationship of trust is developed with them as people.

Hewlett Packard calls this MBWA (Management By Walking Around). I have watched Max DePree walk through the factory at Herman Miller, addressing people by name, asking about family and outside activities, clearly a friend who cares. I like to connect with members of my immediate team regularly just to see how they are doing. In my middle management days, the president would often catch me sitting slumped in a chair talking to one of my staff. Sometimes I think he thought I was loafing. But I consider keeping up relationships with them and maintaining high motivation to be important work since I have delegated so much to them (which is precisely why I have time to sit and chat).

One caution here. The need to socialize and encourage strong relationships cannot be allowed to interfere with the work. Part of having a trusting relationship with the team includes their being able to tell you that this is not a good time to talk if they are to finish the assignment they are working on. Even coaching leaders need to be sensitive about intruding into people's time. A strong trusting relationship, however, will find the proper balance.

Trust is an important component of team unity. The team must trust the leader, and they must know that the leader trusts them. And they must trust each other. James Kouzes and Barry Posner in their excellent book *Credibility* argue that trust is the foundation of leadership.[17] We often talk about trust being earned. But trust is also given, and it is a fragile gift that must be cared for gently.

7. Vulnerability

Team leaders must be vulnerable. They must be open enough for others to learn from their mistakes. It is hard to fail in front of your staff, but it builds trust and community if you are big enough to admit it. I have had to apologize many times. My team members have always known my weaknesses and fears as well as my strengths and dreams. They already know that leaders are not perfect, they are just waiting for us to recognize it!

This was brought home to me sharply in the incident of the water cooler, an incident about which I later wrote a short article for *Leadership*.[18] Several years ago, two programmes for which I was responsible were merged into one office operation, combining staff and reassigning responsibilities. The Doctor of Ministry (DMin) programme staff moved into the office facilities of the Leadership Institute. An excellent team was forged, but there was one problem. The old DMin team had had their own water cooler in their office; the Institute team used one across the hall.

Early in the relocation process, members of the DMin team approached me requesting a water cooler with refrigerator for our office. I pointed out that I did not think this necessary since we had access to one across the hall and were short on space. However, wanting to be a good participative manager, I delegated this decision to the combined members of the new staff team – I told them to do the necessary research and make the decision.

A week later they came to me with a recommendation to buy a certain model of water cooler and handed me the papers that I needed to sign to implement their decision. Again, I expressed my reservations about the project, but signed the papers.

Several days later I walked into the primary reception office for our combined unit and saw a new water cooler boldly bubbling in the corner. I did not like it. From my perspective it turned a professional office reception area into a staff lounge. I told the staff how I felt – basically that I thought they had made a bad decision, reiterating again that we really did not need the water cooler and that it did not fit the 'professional ambience' of the office.

As happens often, this was the point when the leadership role in our office shifted to another member of the team. A person who had worked with me for several years – and who had not even supported the water cooler recommendation – took me aside and confronted my behaviour. She accused me of acting out of character with what I believed and taught. She asked whether I had really delegated the decision or whether I was playing some 'parenting' game expecting the 'children' to make my decision, and when they did not, I was pouting. (These are my words, she was much more loving and discreet!)

She was right! I had not delegated completely. I had delegated the decision only as long as it was done my way. That is not delegation – that is bad management. When I delegated the decision to get a water cooler, I transferred my authority to determine the outcome and placed it in the hands of the staff. It was their decision and my behaviour now denied that I had really delegated the authority to decide.

Fortunately, someone cared enough to confront me and call me to account by my own stated management values. I apologized to the whole team and acknowledged that it was their decision, that I was out of line and that I would support their decision completely. For some of the team this was the first time they had seen a manager apologize. But I was wrong and I needed to say so. That experience greatly strengthened the new team that was coming together. And to this day, I believe, the water cooler is still bubbling and gurgling away as a monument to completed delegation and vulnerable leadership.

8. Delegation

Complete delegation, not water cooler delegation, builds people. It gives them confidence because it says, 'I trust you.' Delegation is the process of moving the decision point from the leader to the follower. It is the act of giving power and authority with responsibility to the follower, allowing him or her to serve as leader for that decision. Max DePree, in his best-selling book *Leadership Jazz*, sees delegation as a gracious act of involvement that grows people, that embraces diversity, that builds on trust and requires a dying to self.[19] Delegation develops ownership and responsibility. I will often say that my job is sitting around drinking coffee and talking to people. This is not totally untrue! If I am doing my job right, I need only be available at the critical points to provide relational support, discussion or direction, when the person who has accepted the delegation wants to talk. When team members accept our delegation, they become leaders and we become resources that they manage as they carry out their delegated responsibility.

9. Ownership of results, not tasks

Team members own the organizational outcomes, the results, not just their own job descriptions. When team members see something that needs to be done in order to accomplish their team goals, they do it, whether it is their job or not. A good team takes pride in the results of their unit as well as their personal contributions. They look for ways to support one another, to fill in the cracks, to do whatever is needed to achieve the results the team is seeking. A good team always keeps the larger picture in view and measures its success by results.

I will come back to this element when I look at vision and planning. Leadership in times of change is increasingly going to require us to focus on results rather than tasks or strategies. Yet it is so easy for our organizations to lock into the way we do things, the tasks or the strategies, as though the strategy is the mission. I will argue that organizations, like effective teams, must focus on a vision of results and be willing to change their strategies as necessary to fulfil their mission.

10. Equality of status

Each member of the team is important. Each person has an area for which they are responsible. They need to know that they are valued. Even though members are paid at different rates for a variety of reasons, each person on the team expects to be treated as equally important to the team – and this includes the leader.

11. Freedom to make mistakes – once

This element we saw in the Peters and Austin list. Mistakes are going to happen, no matter how hard we try to prevent them. Effective leaders do not get the team paranoid about making mistakes. You cannot prevent them all. The principle is to try not to make the same one twice! Learn from mistakes. If people are not making mistakes, they are not trying new things. If they are making the same mistake twice, they are not learning new things! A good team knows that it can take the risk to try, to fail and to learn from its mistakes.

12. Ownership is more important than hours worked
Again, the focus of a team is on results. If the goals or results are owned, they will get done. If the hours clocked are a priority, you may not get the results you need. While team members identified this as an important principle, it is actually implicit in the other points. The focus should be on the ownership of results, not tasks or hours. As flexible hours and telecommuting possibilities are changing the way we work, it will be increasingly important that the focus be on the results of the team efforts.

13. Commitment to a team approach
Fitting into the team becomes an important qualification for a position. The team fit becomes an important element in the hiring process, alongside skills and experience. I have often told new employees that their evaluation will be based on their ability to fit and work as a member of the team as much as it will be on their individual competencies. All members of the team need to know that they belong; they need to feel valued and believe that they have an important contribution to make to the team's success.

These are the elements that one team identified as important to their success. As I mentioned above, these same elements are underscored by much of the current research on team building and work groups. For those working in a local church, Harold Westing has written a valuable *Multiple Church-Staff Handbook*, applying team principles to the local congregation. His basic thesis is that you cannot ask the church to function as a biblical community – a team – if the church leadership is not modelling it.[20]

Servant leaders and coaches thrive in team settings. And teams need servant leaders. In 1976 a team of climbers from the United States was organized to climb Nanda Devi in the Indian Himalaya mountains. One of the organizers of the climb was Willie Unsoeld, a former Everest climber living in Seattle. He arranged the climb to celebrate the 21st birthday of his daughter, Nanda Devi, who would accompany the team to the summit of this 25,645 foot peak after which she had been named. The team was made up of highly skilled climbers, selected because of friendships and extended relationship links. Because they were all friends and because they were all experienced and 'gifted' climbers, no one person was designated as the expedition leader. Senior climbers shared the leadership, carefully deferring to one another in recognition of the community of gifts and abilities present.

Was it a successful expedition? Yes, if success is measured in the accomplishment of their objective. On September 1, 1976, the team placed three climbers on the summit of Nanda Devi. But at what price? As the climbing became more difficult, tempers grew shorter and decisions needed to be made to conserve resources and energy. Yet no one had been assigned the responsibility of seeing that decisions were made and implemented. Shared leadership broke down into disagreement and stalemates. Critical decisions were delayed. Most tragic of all was the case of Nanda Devi Unsoeld, the young woman for whom the trip was organized. When she became ill at a high altitude camp, there was no one to tell her she could not continue the climb, that she had to go back down and recuperate. No individual decision, no group decision. Everyone was nice to Nanda Devi. But she died on the mountain, a victim of a leaderless team of gifted people.

The trip ended on a tragic note. Fingers were pointed, Blame was passed around. Climbers belatedly suggested, 'I should have stepped forward and pushed for a decision.' Everyone was taking care of themselves. No one was taking care of the group. No one was helping the team make the decisions necessary for the accomplishment of its goal and the care of its members. I doubt if any of those climbers ever joined another expedition unless it was clear who was taking responsibility for the care of the group, who had authority to enforce the implementation of the team's decision processes. A gifted team is not enough. A gifted leader is also needed to *serve* the team, to see that the mission is pursued, the people are cared for and the decisions made.[21]

Conclusion: 'If today you will be a servant ...'

To close this chapter, we turn again to a biblical model. In 1 Kings 11 and 12 we see Rehoboam crowned as king of Israel after the death of Solomon. The people were burdened by the harsh rule of Solomon in his later years and sent Jeroboam to plead their case with the new king. Rehoboam told Jeroboam that he would consider the petition and decide in three days. In that time he consulted the senior advisors who had served with Solomon. These elders advised him, 'If you will be a servant to these people and serve them and give them a favourable answer, they will always be your servants.'

But this was not the answer that Rehoboam wanted, so he sought the advice of the young men who had grown up with him. Their counsel was to show himself stronger than his father, to use his power to control and rule the people. Rehoboam followed the advice of his young counsellors. He chose to rule rather than to serve. And it cost him his leadership. Within weeks he had lost 11/12 of his kingdom to Jeroboam. Rehoboam's decision to be a strong leader decimated the scope of this leadership.

As Emilie Griffin writes in *The Reflective Executive*, leaders hold something very fragile in their hands – the hopes and dreams and ideas and contributions of their people. These must be held gently with respect, not crushed in the fist of power.[22]

> 'If you will be a servant to these people and serve them ...
> they will always be your servants.'

Notes

[1] Herman Hesse, *The Journey to the East* (New York: Noonday Press, 1956), 98. It is with this story that Robert Greenleaf launches his foundational work *Servant Leadership*, 1977.
[2] Thomas J. Peters and Robert H. Waterman, Jr., *In Search of Excellence* (New York: Harper & Row, 1982).
[3] Gary A. Yukl, *Leadership in Organizations* (Englewood Cliffs, N.J.: Prentice Hall, 1981), 3. See also Howard Gardner, *Leading Minds* (New York: Basic Books, 1996), 8–9.
[4] Paul Hersey and Kenneth H. Blanchard, *Management of Organizational Behavior* (Englewood Cliffs, N.J.: Prentice Hall, 1988), 5.
[5] John W. Gardner, *On Leadership* (New York: Free Press, 1990), 2.
[6] Yukl, *Leadership*, 10–17.
[7] Hersey and Blanchard, *Management*, 171.
[8] James O'Toole, *Leading Change* (San Francisco: Jossey-Bass, 1995), 7–8, worries that contingency leadership allows leaders to default to their most comfortable directive style whenever they find themselves in a complex or difficult situation, which is most of the time. When this happens, O'Toole says, contingency leadership is ineffective.
[9] Jack O. Balswick and Walter C. Wright, Jr., 'A Complementary–Empowering Model of Ministerial Leadership', in J.I. Packer (ed.), *The Best in Theology*, vol. 4 (Carol Stream, Ill.: Christianity Today, 1990), 323.
[10] James MacGregor Burns, *Leadership* (New York: Harper & Row, 1978), 4.
[11] Peter Block, *The Empowered Manager* (San Francisco: Jossey-Bass, 1987), 15.
[12] This story was told by Max DePree in a public lecture and is used with his permission.
[13] The movie *Schindler's List* is another graphic presentation of this kind of empowering leadership.
[14] Tom Peters and Nancy Austin, *A Passion for Excellence* (New York: Warner Books, 1989).
[15] I first heard this story from Max DePree, who heard Don Shula tell it at an event in Puerto Rico.
[16] Gardner, *Leadership*, 10.
[17] James M. Kouzes and Barry Z. Posner, *Credibility* (San Francisco: Jossey-Bass, 1993), 22.

18 Walter C. Wright, Jr., 'Watercooler Management', *Leadership* 10, 2 (1989), 132.
19 Max DePree, *Leadership Jazz* (New York: Doubleday, 1992), 157.
20 Harold Westing, *Multiple Church-Staff Handbook* (Grand Rapids: Kregel, 1985), 16.
21 The story is told poignantly in John Roskelly, *Nanda Devi* (Harrisburg, Penn.: Stackpole Books, 1987).
22 Emilie Griffin, *The Reflective Executive* (New York: Crossroad, 1993), 53.

Chapter III

Vision and Hope

Clouds: Delivering Vision

'Clouds without rain, blown along by the wind.' Again we return to Jude's challenging of the leadership of those who claimed to be leaders in his community. In his powerful metaphor of the cloud, promising rain and refreshment to a parched land but delivering only wind, we again see two contrasting pictures of a Christian leader.

The picture Jude paints to describe the non-leaders shows them holding out hope but having nothing to offer. They promise leadership but care only for themselves. It is not hard to see them in their pulpits, on their pedestals, gesturing with energy and passion but without content. They offer no lasting vision, no hope. They have no concept of a future that binds the community together. Rather they divide and polarize the people. These leaders do not point to the power of God's presence in Christ but only to their own piety and personal spiritual pilgrimage.

On the other hand, we see Jude, the servant leader, pointing away from himself to God in Christ, serving his people by lifting up a compelling vision to give them hope. Listen again to the hope-filled words of his benediction:

To him who is able to keep you from falling and to present you before his glorious presence without fault and with great joy – to the only God, our Saviour be glory, majesty, power and authority, through Jesus Christ our Lord, before all ages, now and forevermore. (Jude 25)

Now that is a vision to stir the heart! Jude sees the future – and it is God's!

> Leadership is about vision that empowers.

Now, let us look again at the Colossian drama and see what difference vision makes. This time put yourself in Philemon's place.

Philemon: Implementing Vision

How would you feel? You are a recognized leader in your church. A person respected for the care and commitment you shower on others in your congregation. You actively participate in and support the development of community in your church fellowship. People are refreshed in their faith because of your leadership and the depth of your relationship with Christ.

But you've had some problems lately. A member of your personal staff has betrayed you. A person you trusted has stolen from you and left town. Which hurts worse – the loss of a good worker, the theft of your property, or the betrayal by someone to whom you gave your trust? This event has not affected your vision, your leadership in the church, but it has hurt you personally. Perhaps you still carry a little anger, maybe a lot of anger! You were betrayed. Now you understand a little of what Jesus felt when Judas turned against him.

Judas was part of Jesus' inner circle, a disciple of the Lord. A person chosen by Jesus in answer to his prayer to God for twelve disciples. Jesus trusted Judas. Jesus loved Judas. And Judas betrayed Jesus. He violated that relationship of trust and turned on the one who loved him. You feel some of what

Jesus must have felt when the person he had chosen, the person he trusted, turned on him. What are you going to do about these feelings that you have?

Then one morning you look up and see two men coming towards you. One is the thief. How do you feel? What emotions run through your mind? Revenge? Repayment? Justice? Your fist clenches. Your stomach tightens. Your heart speeds up. Now finally you can take care of this matter that has been eating at you – this hurt and anger that you have been carrying around.

But who is this other guy? Isn't that someone you've seen with Paul? Tychicus, I think his name was. What's he doing here? Perhaps he found out about that scoundrel and has dragged him back here to see justice done. And yet something seems wrong here as Tychicus greets you on behalf of himself and Paul. Your runaway staff member is watching you with a strange look in his eyes – a mixture of love and sadness. But not fear. Why not? You can have his head for what he did to you.

And then Tychicus hands you the letter – a personal letter from Paul who is in prison in Ephesus.

Paul, a prisoner of Christ Jesus, and Timothy our brother,

To Philemon our dear friend and fellow worker, to Apphia our sister, to Archippus our fellow soldier and to the church that meets in your home.

Grace to you and peace from God our Father and the Lord Jesus Christ.

I always thank my God as I remember you in my prayers, because I hear about your faith in the Lord Jesus and your love for all the saints. I pray that you may participate actively in the fellowship of your faith[1] so that you will have a full understanding of every good thing we have in Christ.

Your love has given me great joy and encouragement, because you, brother, have refreshed the hearts of the saints. Therefore, although in Christ I could be bold and order you to do what you ought to do, yet I appeal to you on the basis of love. I then, as Paul – an old man and now also a prisoner of Christ Jesus – I appeal to you for my son Onesimus, who became my son while I was in chains. Formerly he was useless to you, but now he has become useful both to you and to me.

I am sending him – who is my very heart – back to you. I would have liked to keep him with me so that he could take your place in helping me while I am in chains for the gospel. But I did not want to do anything without your consent, so that any favour you do will be spontaneous and not forced. Perhaps the reason he was separated from you for a little while was that you might have him back for good – no longer as a slave, but better than a slave, as a dear fellow believer. He is very dear to me but even dearer to you, both as a person and as a fellow believer in the Lord.

So if you consider me a partner, welcome him as you would welcome me. If he has done you any wrong or owes you anything, charge it to me. I, Paul, am writing this with my own hand. I will pay it back – not to mention that you owe me your very self. I do wish, brother, that I may have some benefit from you in the Lord; refresh my heart in Christ. Confident of your obedience, I write to you, knowing that you will do even more than I ask.

And one thing more: Prepare a guest room for me, because I hope to be restored to you in answer to your prayers.

Epaphras, my fellow prisoner in Christ Jesus, sends you greetings. And so do Mark, Aristarchus, Demas and Luke, my fellow workers.

The grace of the Lord Jesus Christ be with your spirit. (Philemon)

Subtly, lovingly, but clearly, Paul is sending you a message. Things have changed with Onesimus your runaway slave. He is now a Christian brother. Everything that you have been teaching and preaching at church, sharing with your friends at work, is suddenly being put to the test. Participation in the fellowship of *koinonia* is no longer a lofty personal vision. It is no longer a theoretical theological concept of our common fellowship in Christ. It is now a demanding expectation of your faith. What you have been teaching as a commitment of your faith and an expression of your vision, you are now being asked to demonstrate in relationship to a person who has betrayed your trust.

It's as though Paul is saying, 'Okay Philemon, let's see if you really believe what you have been talking about. *Your vision should make a difference in your life.* Now is the time to see if that works. Reinstate Onesimus, not just back on your staff but also as a Christian brother. This is your chance to model what you believe!'

With a masterful stroke of his pen, Paul has confronted Philemon with the implications of his vision and stated commitments. The Christian love for which he is so well known all comes down now to how he will deal with Onesimus. Paul expects the gospel to make a difference. He is confident that Philemon will be able to transcend his sense of offence, his personal loss and his pain at betrayal, and embrace Onesimus as a changed person and a Christian companion, reinstating him to his staff and taking the risk of trusting him again.

Philemon knew his faith. He had a vision of what it means to live for Christ, what it means to be part of the body of Christ. He had a reputation for goodness and piety. But Paul wanted more. Paul had a theological vision for an eschatological community in Christ that shaped everything he did. He wanted Philemon's vision to permeate his total being in such as way that it changed the way he lived. A vision that makes a difference. It's one thing to have a vision for Christian community. It's another to see Jesus in the eyes of the person who has betrayed your trust and hurt you personally. For Paul, one leads to the other. A biblical vision, according to Paul, results in changed lives in everyday living. Everything that Philemon taught about his faith was now on the line in the way he responded to Onesimus.

The same holds true for each of us. Vision is seeing tomorrow so powerfully that it shapes today. Our vision of God in Christ at work in the communities and organizations that we lead will be put to the test every day in the way we live, the way we do business, the way we parent, the way we walk with friends or relate to strangers. An empowering vision of community means meeting God in the context of a community united in Christ.

In his carefully worded letter to Philemon, Paul tells us at least three things about his vision of community that we should note as we seek to be servant leaders.

Christian community includes all kinds of people

For Philemon, this was a dramatic revelation. A person who was once his slave, he must now see as a Christian brother in the community. What will this mean? How does an upper-middle-class church leader relate to an uneducated runaway slave? But this is the essence of Christian community. We are a diverse fellowship of uniquely gifted people. Together we become the body of Christ pointing people to God.

This diversity will take different forms in various communities. At Regent College we welcome students, faculty and staff from over 32 different countries and cultures, 75 different church or denominational backgrounds, a variety of vocations, a mixture of ages and experience, and different levels of socio-economic opportunity. This is diversity.

In his book *Leadership is an Art* Max DePree calls this the 'inclusive perspective' of leadership. If we believe 'that every person brings an offering to a group, it requires us to include as many people as possible'.[2] Leaders are *inclusive*, looking for ways to promote diversity and create space for people to develop their unique contribution.

I believe that diversity is an essential ingredient in Christian community. But diversity means differences; and differences produce conflict. And that brings me to the second point I find in Paul's vision and another reason why I find the Colossian story so compelling.

Christian community can handle conflict

It is in community that conflict is reconciled. Paul has certain expectations for Philemon and the Colossian church in relationship to the conflict that Philemon has with Onesimus. His vision of community does not avoid conflict. He addresses it head on in the context of a caring relationship. In fact, I believe Paul's letter to Philemon outlines a very powerful approach to conflict resolution. I will explore conflict in community a little more when we look at values.

> Leaders accept and manage conflict.

Christian community takes precedence over personal agendas

The expectation that this will happen is the third element I
see in Paul's vision for community. We began this chapter by
looking at Philemon's feelings. He has a debt to settle with
Onesimus, a personal agenda to take care of. Yet Paul is
calling him back to his vision of community. Paul reminds
him of his reputation for investing himself in the network of
relationships that form his community and for encouraging
its members – his faith, his love and his generous support for
the community at Colosse. Now Paul sends Onesimus back
as a member of that community – and expects Philemon's
vision of community to take precedence over his own hurt,
his own need for personal satisfaction.

Organizations are communities of diversity. They are filled
with individuals with their own issues. Regent College is a
community of over 500 personal agendas. Early in my tenure
at Regent, I heard a professor comment that what made
Regent different from other schools at which he had taught
was the willingness of faculty members to submit their strong
personal agendas to the community agenda of the college. I
pray that will always be true at Regent. It should be true for
any organization that holds up a vision of Christian community.

Max DePree would go further and apply these same prin-
cipals to Herman Miller. He writes:

> In a group like Herman Miller, we have both personal diversity and
> corporate diversity. When we think of *corporate* diversity, we think
> about the gifts and talents and commitment that each of us as individ-
> uals bring to the group effort. Channeled correctly and integrated
> properly, our diversity can be our greatest strength. But there is always
> the temptation to use these gifts for our personal benefit rather than
> dedicating them to the best interest of the group.[3]

Leadership, DePree would argue, articulates a vision for the
organization or community that is inclusive – creating space
for individual gifts and talents, and creating the context that
allows these individual offerings to be integrated for the
good of the group and its mission together.

Paul has such a vision. His vision for Christian community in Colosse embraces diversity, deals with conflict and supersedes individual agendas. He expects that vision to make a difference in the immediate day-to-day relationships of living. That is the vision to which he calls Philemon. And that is the vision by which he would critique all of our plans for the future

> Leaders have visions that make a difference, empowering visions that offer hope for tomorrow and shape behaviours today.

The Responsibilities of Leadership

In his book *Leadership is an Art* Max DePree says that the two primary responsibilities of a leader are to point the direction or define reality and to say thank you.[4] For DePree, leaders articulate the vision, that is, they point the direction and define the reality which shapes both the leadership relationship and the followers' contributions to the organization. However, he recognizes immediately that the vision articulated by the leader will only be accomplished with the contributions of those followers. Thus he sees the second responsibility of leadership as saying thank you – acknowledging our dependence upon and appreciation for the followers and their personal investment in the vision.

Whenever I am asked what my job is, I like to elaborate on DePree's primary responsibilities by responding with four things which, I believe, define my leadership role at Regent College. I am responsible for articulating the vision, reinforcing the values, empowering the people and saying thanks. Obviously the first and last are taken directly from DePree. The middle two are also consistent with his writing in all three of his leadership books.

In this chapter I focus on articulating the vision – articulating an *empowering vision* that shapes the way we organize our corporate life together around a mission. In the next chapter I will pick up the second responsibility and talk about the crucial role of the leader in creating and reinforcing the *empowering values* that, when embedded in our organizational cultures, shape the way we live our community life together. In Chapter 5 I will focus on the *empowering relationships* in which we contextualize the contributions of our people in terms of our mission, and, as DePree would say, 'abandon ourselves to their giftedness'.[5] In Chapter 6 I will conclude with a review of *empowering accountability* which includes the dependent accountability of leaders to their followers – the men and women who with the leader share a compelling vision that shapes their relationships together.

Planning: Visions of Hope

Planning is the management process of lifting up visions of hope in times of change. Planning is the process of articulating a strategic vision or picture of the future in a way that compels others to take ownership for that future and understand why their contribution is important. One critical component of our role as leaders is to keep our organizations thinking strategically about who we are and what we want to accomplish before God. This strategic thinking or planning shapes the daily life and work of our organizations and directs the energies of our people. It shapes the direction and character of the organization in such a way that people are empowered to make their contribution and valued for that contribution. Planning articulates purpose, meaning and hope in the living of a shared vision.

Defining strategic planning

We need to start this discussion with some definitions. Every planning text uses terms like purpose, mission, goals, objectives, actions, strategies, budgets, controls. However, the chances are high that if you choose two texts, you will get different definitions for these terms. 'Purpose' and 'mission' are frequently interchanged. 'Goals' and 'objectives' are either used synonymously or one (either one) is defined as the broader target with the other as the specific measurable benchmark.

Strategic planning tends to be the current label for what used to be called long-range planning. Some authors try to distinguish between strategic planning and long-range planning, but without much success. Generally speaking, long-range planning focuses on the time frame involved, something increasingly difficult to control in our changing times, while strategic planning focuses on the issues at stake.

I like to define strategic planning as *a process initiated by the top leadership of an organization to review and monitor the purpose, the mission, the values or culture, and the strategies of the organization.* Let's look at the components of this definition.

Purpose is the primary role of the organization as defined by society and shared with other organizations. Regent College and Fuller Seminary share a similar purpose. First Baptist Church and Fairview Presbyterian Church share a similar purpose. Apple Computers and IBM share a similar purpose.

Mission, on the other hand, refers to the unique calling or distinctive of each organization that defines that organization by geography, values, beliefs, services, resources, size, people served, etc. It is what makes you different from every other similar organization with the same purpose. Your mission is what gives you a right to exist and utilize resources. It answers the question: What would be lost if we ceased to exist?

By *values and culture* I am referring to the stated or assumed beliefs, commitments, ethos or qualities that govern everything that the organization does – the character of the organization, if you will, the manifestation of its soul, its faith and beliefs. This is the part that gets left out of most planning processes. Since I believe that values are as much a part of vision as mission, I want to come back to this unique responsibility of leadership in detail in the next chapter.

Strategies I define as unified sets of goals, including objectives and actions, that move us towards the accomplishment of the organizational mission and values given our current and projected resources, opportunities and threats. I choose here to avoid talking about specific goals, objectives and actions in order to keep us looking at the packages we put together to implement our mission and values.

Every September in Vancouver, the streets are blocked off and sounds of roaring engines fill the city. The Molson Indy pits world-class teams against one another as their cars race through downtown corridors. Drivers and crews are on the news and are the topic of most conversations during this long weekend. Each team is working out and discussing its strategies to finish first on race day. They are talking about much more than goals and objectives. It is when these elements are unified in a way that controls our actions that we have a strategy! Racing drivers do not carry a list of key objectives in the car to check off after each lap. Rather they live and drive their strategy. In today's fast-paced world, we lead like racing-car drivers. We do not have a strategy for achieving our mission until we have melded the various steps together into a way of life for the organization over the next few years.

There are two additional key components in this definition of strategic planning

Strategic planning is a *process*. The involvement of people is as important as the production of a plan. The plan shows that something was accomplished, and it also becomes the control document with which to evaluate the organization's progress. The process, though, involves people and creates ownership. It translates the shared vision into the commitments and actions of the members of the organization. This very strength of planning is why planning is so difficult. The process involves people – people with their own ideas, dreams and plans. Planning for one person is easy. As soon as you add a second person it becomes difficult, but absolutely essential if you want ownership of the vision and the strategies. The more people you involve in the planning process, the longer it will take and the harder it will be. But it is critical to the ownership and motivation of the people.

I should note here that I am talking about process, not democracy. In strategic planning we need participation to advise the decision makers and develop ownership. Participants in the planning process, however, do not necessarily have an equal vote in shaping the future – that depends on the particular culture of your organization – but they do participate and contribute to the decisions that the leadership is responsible for making. The process is both the problem and also the foundational principle of planning.

Finally, *top management* must be the ones to initiate strategic planning. You will hear arguments for top-down planning and bottom-up planning. The middle manager does not want to waste time planning until the president shares her vision, since 'that's what we are going to do anyway'. The president does not want to form her vision before hearing the ideas of the middle management. In either case, the leadership must be involved. The top leadership is responsible for the decisions that move the organization into the future – the allocation of resources and the delegation of authority to make things happen. If the president or pastor does not own the planning process, it is a waste of everyone's time!

Strategic planning, then, is a process initiated by the leadership that clarifies the organization's mission, within its basic purpose; that identifies the values that will govern the way the organization or church lives out its mission; that translates the mission and values into vision statements or scenarios for the future; and develops strategies to turn those scenarios into reality, including goals, objectives, actions and budgets. Mission – values – strategies: these are the key components of strategic planning, the vital issues that leaders must constantly keep before their organizations in times of change.

Planning in times of change

Before we look at a planning model and the development of empowering vision statements, let's look briefly at some of the change swirling around us.

I like to read Charles Handy. His two books on organizational change, *The Age of Unreason* and *The Age of Paradox*, stimulate me to approach things from a fresh perspective, to think outside the lines.[6] Handy argues that we have moved into a time of discontinuous change. Change comes so fast from so many directions that we cannot extrapolate into the future with any certainty. Apart from the foundation of our faith, the only constant Handy will allow us to take into the future is that it will change.[7] In the world of tomorrow, 'built to last now means built to change'.[8] He argues, as did Tom Peters in *Thriving on Chaos*, that with all this change bombarding individuals and organizations we have to plan within a context we experience as chaos. It has become more critical than ever, claims Russ Chandler in his book *Racing Toward 2001*, for Christians to know who they are and with whom they are entering this chaotic future.[9]

Trajectories we set for ourselves as youths are no longer valid for many of us, not to mention for our children, or for our students, employees or congregations. This is already clear in theological education. The students who seek theological study today are different from those who came to us ten years ago. In a world swirling with change, they are entering theological studies asking: Who am I? What should I be doing with my life?

Let me outline some of the changes that organizational planners and futurists predict will affect us in this decade. The forces for change include changing values, changing technology, the changing shape of relationships, changing attitudes towards education, changing attitudes towards work and changing attitudes towards faith. (Again, I must make a disclaimer here. My information is based on Western, predominantly North American, research and writing.)

1. Changing values
Of all the changes swirling round us, changing values may have the greatest impact on our leadership. The following shifts in values are already being experienced, and will increase over the next decade:

- *From quantity of possessions to quality of possessions*
  Most futurists see 'quality' as a key value for the future, partly from increased global awareness and partly from individual pampering.[10]

- *From value of money to value of time*
  Time will be the top currency of the future. It will be the asset we have that is most sought after by others.[11] Already we will pay for ways to save time – using technology, paying others to do labour-intensive work for us. And this goes along closely with another value shift.

- *From satisfaction through work to satisfaction through leisure*
  Time will be protected for discretionary activities. Work will become less central to defining a person's identity, with leisure and voluntary service replacing remunerated work as the way we express who we are. This trend can already be seen as more and more people work shorter hours and build work around their recreational or volunteer activities. It has been projected that by 2000 less than half the workforce in North America will be in traditional 'full-time' jobs. People will be designing life packages or portfolios of part-time and piecework or services.[12]

  Recently I was with three sets of friends, one couple in their 30s, one in their 40s, and one in the 50s. Each of them had already moved into this portfolio mode. The lawyer had cut back to four days per week, working out of his home so he could be more involved with church volunteer work. The psychologist had just reduced his schedule from four days per week to three so he could travel and look for something new to do. The corporation president had sold his business, bought several commercial properties and now serves as the manager and handyman for them, working about five hours per day. The line between work and leisure is blurring.

- *From old traditions to new traditions*
  Or as one psychologist put it, from convention or conformity to conviction. Just because it was done one way in the past, or by my parents, or is the way churches, schools and organizations usually work is no reason why it must be the way we do it now. People will increasingly do things

because they choose to, not because they are supposed to. We will do things we believe in, not things we are told or expected to do. Partly this may reflect a distrust in the traditions that have been handed down, and partly it may be a response to changing realities around us.

A corollary to this may be a greater tolerance for diversity as each person's convictions are respected. However, even as I see this leading to a workable pluralism in North American society, I also see increased fragmentation, with diversity producing hostility. It may be difficult to maintain a balance.

- *From commitment to flexibility*
  Even as we adjust to people choosing from conviction rather than tradition, we have to recognize a tendency to avoid long-term commitments. This is partly in response to the ambiguity of continual change and partly out of a need to protect the personal resource of time. There will be a desire to keep things open and flexible, with short-term commitments and contracts.

  An interesting corollary that brings together values related to time, leisure and lack of commitment is the expectation that the more different experiences one has, the more likely one will be to find fulfilment, and the more valuable one will be as a resource. Consequently, people will allocate shorter blocks of time to any single activity. Mission agencies already report an increase in interest in short-term missions over career missionary commitments. A recent article in *Fast Company* goes so far as to propose that organizational recruiters should focus on the experiences that candidates have accumulated. Who have they worked for, who have they worked with, what have they worked on?[13]

- *From group identity to individualism*
  This is already clearly visible in the United States in an increased distrust of organizations and the assertion of individuals' rights. In Canada the focus seems to be more on the distrust of organizations than on individual rights. But what will this mean for organizations? for churches,

for schools? Esther Dyson, a consultant to the computer industry, is convinced that within five years we will see the balance of power shift from organizations, owners and managers to individual contributors. Individuals will shape organizations, not let organizations shape them.[14]

- *From trusting people to proven integrity*
The final value change brings us back to the quality issue. Integrity and character will be key issues in a world where things are changing so fast you do not know whom or what to trust. Trust will have to be earned and it will be prized as a mark of character.

2. Changing technology
In many ways, changing technology is influencing everything else. Stephen Covey laments the shift he already sees away from character and values to technique and technology.[15] Technology is being used to free up time and we will gladly pay the cost. The telephone, computer, FAX machine, e-mail and the World Wide Web have redefined geographical boundaries and organizational walls. More and more work is done by telecommuting, at home or on the road. Organizations now have to think about *anytime anyplace*.[16]

Information is now available immediately. Nearly every magazine these days has an article on the growth of the Internet as a means of communication and connectivity. The Internet has removed time and space constraints. Information overload and informed use of information already present problems.

Education will be impacted heavily by technology. Librarians hate to hear me say this, but I believe that we are only short years away from computer databases replacing the traditional library. Once this happens, our teaching locations will no longer be tied to specific research centres. Already I buy books from Amazon.com, get the news from CNN.com, and because I am planning a trip to Nepal, receive daily issues of the *Kathmandu Post* by e-mail. If I have a question, I go to the Internet first. Information, courses and even degrees are available over the internet. What does that mean for education?

Technology is also producing the generation that gathers information from the 8-second 'sound bite' used so effectively on TV news – a brief clip that captures the speaker's message. We are looking for written or visual distillations of vast quantities of information, packaged in small bites by a trusted interpreter. Each week the Kiplinger letter, a weekly business newsletter out of Washington, D.C., outlines the world in four pages for thousands who have learned to trust Austin Kiplinger's selection of news. I have listened to the editor of a prominent Christian journal lament that the younger pastor or seminarian does not take time to read. In the church setting, long sermons make younger families restless. Too much information. We want it broken down into chunks that we can handle. As church consultant, Lyle Schaller says, we look for a trusted messenger to interpret which information we need to hear. Television news teams invest heavily in creating an anchor reporter who develops trust relationships with an audience because most of us prefer to hear the news from someone whose interpretation we have learned to value. Schaller believes we are moving into a future in which the messenger may become more important than the message.[17] All of this raises serious questions about education and about the ministry of the church. How will people learn in this next decade? How do we facilitate that learning in our theological schools? How do we adapt our teaching methods to the learning methods of the world we seek to educate? What form must the church take for people to hear God's word and participate in vital Christian community?

3. Changing relationships

Planners see an increasing shift from the traditional family to single-parent families, blended families, cohabiting adults, even street gangs. Divorce and multiple marriages are seen as the norm in North America, compounded by a rapid increase in the number of multi-generational households. Already children are leaving home at a later age and many are returning with all or part of a family. Loneliness will be widespread as individualized work and withdrawal from participation in

organizations displace usual sources for developing friendships and individual-focused people forget the skills of maintaining friendships. Couple the loss of relational skills with
the reluctance to commit and we will see a troubled time for
relationships in the years ahead.

This presents an immediate challenge for leadership, since
the Information Age – which some think is already half
over[18] – is about an economic web of relationships. Connectivity, the lifeblood of the Internet, is about relationships.
Relationships form the foundation of our living together –
they are what being human is all about – but as individuals
turn in on themselves and lose the concept of service to one
another, the intimacy of friendship is at risk. Relationship
displaces friendship when relationships are seen as part of
your knowledge base, part of your personal capital,[19] when
the other person becomes the object of business rather than
a friend. Christian leaders will be part of the connected web
of organizational relationships even as they nurture community and friendships. As I noted above, leadership is a relationship. It must be a relationship that bridges the functional
connectedness of the organization and the caring interdependence of the community. Leaders may have an important
role in defining *relationship* in the years ahead.

4. Changing attitudes towards education
The future will see an increased focus on learning rather
than on education. Lifelong learning will replace the
concept of completed education; we will never know
enough. There will be more interest in continuous learning
to cope with change than in study to earn a degree. Degrees
may lose their cash value, but education will be critical for
the decisions necessary to manage one's life. More older
people will return to college as society focuses less on youth
and more on redesigning the environment to facilitate
comfort and convenience. Peter Drucker in his book *Post-
Capitalist Society* argues that the educated person of tomorrow must be a balance of the intellectual and the manager –
a person capable of applying knowledge for the benefit of
the world.[20]

5. *Changing attitudes towards work*

As we already noted, there will be a shift from work as identity to work as income and contribution. There will be a definite shift away from single career paths to multiple careers. Talent will be mobile and job tenures short. Most people will move through several careers in their lifetime. There will be a move from full-time work to a 'portfolio' of jobs. Handy sees more part-time and contracted services and volunteer activities being pieced together in a portfolio of commitments.[21] There will be more people working at home, more telecommuting, with work environments at some distance from the home office. There will be more women in leadership roles. The new styles of leadership needed to manage and nurture a network of knowledge workers are thought to be more natural to women.[22] And there will be increased expectation that the work should be designed for the convenience of the employee. No one expects the company to take care of employees for life anymore. So we need to take care of ourselves, and the company needs to fit into that pattern if it wants us to work there. Increasingly I see articles about 'Me, Inc.' or the worker as free agent. If the prophets of business are correct, that will be the trend of the future.

Jeremy Rifkin foresees increased unemployment as people are displaced by technology. Men and women will be forced into a variety of new combinations of salaried work and volunteerism as we rethink how to enable them to participate in the productive benefits of the economy without the traditional access to work, and how to help them find meaning in their contributions.[23] It seems clear that some people with knowledge and ability will be in great demand as we move into the next century. They will be the free agents, capable of negotiating desirable contracts. Yet there will be many who will find themselves washed into an eddy as this river of change rushes past. The world of work is going to get more complicated as men and women try to find personal expression and financial security and keep up with change.[24]

A note should be made here about the work of ministry. The commencement speaker at a prominent Canadian seminary recently warned the graduates heading into parish ministry that they were no longer entering a profession of status in North American society. The church has been marginalized in North America.[25] Neither the church, the pastor nor the seminary can claim any status in the world today. This will increasingly create a major ambiguity about the role of the minister in the church and the church in society.

6. Changing attitudes towards faith
There will be greater tolerance for diversity. Even among Christians, the challenge of the future, according to John Stott, will be to maintain the uniqueness of Christ in a world where all faiths and religions will have equal acceptance or rejection.

More interest will be focused on the local scene than the international. The North American church may find itself focused more on urban mission in North America than on traditional overseas missions. Support will go to what can be locally 'owned' and participated in. We see this already with communities pressing for 'local' forms of theological education supported by local funding.

Yet even as they project the decline of traditional religious structures, there is a strong increase in the search for meaning, for a personal spirituality, a personal spiritual experience. Secularity will continue to dominate, but as Darrell Guder says, people will be 'spiritual secularists'.[26] They will be searching for a faith that gives hope and joy in a time of change and uncertainty. The mission of the church will have to be renewed and reformed into new structures to live for Christ in this changing world.

The future will be a time of change. For many it will be a time of trauma, since change involves loss and loss must be grieved. But the future also offers exciting opportunity. As Christian leaders, we know the one constant that people are searching for in a time of chaos and change – a relationship with God in Christ, which should bring hope and joy and optimism about the future.

The question is, will we be able to revise our vision and modify our strategies when necessary to address this changing future?

Planning is about living the vision

Articulating the vision may be the single most important
responsibility that a leader has. The leader keeps the vision,
the mission, the reason the church or organization was
formed before the people, continually asking what do we
need to do today and tomorrow to live out that vision.

Recently I spent three days with an economist at the University of Calgary. Like most leadership writers, he believes
that we have entered a new paradigm. You can no longer
predict what will happen tomorrow based on traditional economic or planning models. You cannot extrapolate from the
present to the future with any predictability. Basically he is
pessimistic. People are afraid. They see the economy offering
little security to their future. They see violence increasing.
They see an alienated youth culture with increasing openness
to suicide. They see morality floundering rootless. They need
hope! This is the role of vision, of planning, in the context of
our corporations, churches and organizations.

Planning, management and technology cannot bring about
the future, and may not even ensure a better future. At our
best, we will fall short of the ideal. But it can help us understand who we are and what is important to us. It can lift our
attention up from our feet to the horizon and help us see a
vision of a world in which God is at work. Perhaps still a
world that seems to be falling apart when measured by what
we are used to, but a world in which God is still working!
And a world in which we are still called to live out the loving
presence of Christ in our midst.

Jürgen Moltmann, the German theologian, said, that planning offers hope, that planning is our attempt to shape
history in a Godward direction.[27] I am not sure how much
we can shape history, but I do think we are called to live what
we believe, being true to who we are, or better, being true to
who God is in the midst of the changing world.

We need a renewed vision for our leadership that offers
hope that shapes character, providing direction and declaring
worth to the people we seek to influence. This is true regardless of the kind of organization we lead.

A Planning Model

One of the key responsibilities of leadership is the articulation of vision – pointing people to a future that compels them forward towards tomorrow and shapes their living today. Let me suggest a practical model for strategic planning and focus particularly on the development of a scenario or vision statement.

The planning model that shapes my thinking is a simple list of ten questions, which if wrestled with and owned by an organization will create both a vision and a plan for the implementation of that vision. The ten steps to the vision are:

1. Who are we?
2. What is important to us?
3. Where in the world are we?
4. Where do we want to be?
5. What can we do?
6. How should we do it?
7. When will we do it?
8. Who will do it?
9. How are we doing?
10. Was God pleased?

The first four questions, I believe, are the questions of strategic planning. The next four are the questions of operational planning or management, and the last two are the questions of review and evaluation. The ten questions are sequential and cyclical so that the data received from questions nine and ten bring us back again to questions one, two and three. Let's walk through these ten steps.

Who are we? (Strategic planning)

The first task of leadership is to articulate the vision of the organization and that starts with the mission. What is your mission? The mission is the unique calling or distinctive of the organization that defines it by geography or locations, by values, by beliefs, by services offered, by resources accumulated, by constituencies served, etc. The mission is that which makes you different from every other organization like you, that explains why you utilize the resources you do.

1. What is a mission statement?

The mission statement is a concise description of your organization that identifies your primary goals and your distinctives. It answers the fundamental questions: Who are we? What do we do? What do we want to do? Maybe even, how do we do it? It is the final measure or standard against which all organizational decisions and activities are measured. It is a statement of your reason to exist.

Can you articulate your distinctives? Can you write a one-paragraph mission statement today for your organization or church that would distinguish you from everyone else? A mission statement that gives *you* hope and excites you to ministry? A mission statement that the people of your organization would recognize as a statement of their mission too?

2. Why have a mission statement?

First, *it clarifies who we are*. It is the charter or mandate around which the church or organization organizes itself. It tells how the organization or church, as one unique community, fits into the greater scheme of things. Edgar Schein, author of *Organizational Culture and Leadership*, suggests that the mission statement addresses the ultimate survival problem of organizations. It identifies that which is critical to our existence, the loss of which we could not accept.[28] We would rather go out of business than give it up. The mission statement identifies our competitive arena and gives a confidence in our identity that allows cooperation with other organizations and churches. I am frequently concerned by the fear Christians have of cooperation with other institutions of the kingdom who believe differently in matters of faith, lifestyle or social application. A strong sense of mission identity allows an organization to participate in cooperative diversity without fear of losing its distinctive.

Second, the mission statement is *the final goal or standard by which all organizational decisions, all budget and staffing allocations are evaluated.* All planning spins off from the mission. It is the core of all strategy development. If I give you $500,000 to start something new, how will you decide how to use the money? The mission statement guides the planning and implementation processes. It guides decisions regarding size and shape. It tells us which opportunities or threats must be addressed. It should answer the question: How do you measure your success or faithfulness? By identifiable results or by survival?

Third, the mission statement *gives meaning to those who serve in the organization.* It gives value or purpose to their work. It gives direction to their activities, a sense of fit or belonging. It becomes the core of the culture that forms as the organization matures. It answers the question: What will be accomplished if I invest myself in your mission?

Fourth, the mission statement *communicates to those outside the organization.* It reveals who you are to those who utilize your services and participate in your ministries, to those organizations with whom you work, to those who fund your programmes and services.

Organizationally, the mission statement is the foundation of the vision. Leaders hold up a vision of the mission shaped by the organization's values and wrapped in results that make a difference.

3. What makes a good mission statement?
It should be concise, readable and understandable and less than one page. It should not be etched in stone. While it will not be changed continuously, the statement needs to be reviewed regularly and changed when appropriate. It should answer some basic questions about the organization. *Why do we exist?* What need do we address? What 'business' are we in? We tend to focus on what we do rather than the results we want to accomplish. Management books have long critiqued the railroads at this point, noting that railroad companies believed they were in the business of trains when they should have been in the transportation business. Japanese

Acts 2: 42-47

auto companies clearly have transportation as their mission. Some have 250-year strategic plans with groups talking now about travel between planets. Or closer to home: Is your church a preaching station or an equipping centre? We also have a tendency to keep doing what we have done well without asking if it still meets a need. Are you in the business of making buggy whips or starters for moving vehicles? A good mission statement will keep pointing us to the need we are addressing and enable us to resist the temptation to focus on what we are doing now as our mission.

At the same time, the statement should answer the question: *What do we do?* This may well be your distinctive. But if what you do is make buggy whips, you will have a shrinking opportunity for service! What is our most important product or service? Education? Worship? Caring? Evangelism? Social concern? Equipping? Preaching? Widgets? What is our driving force? What are our other services? What else might we want to do? Is there something else we should be doing?

Who are we serving? Who are our customers? Churches struggle with this one. Do we serve the denomination, the members of the congregation, the clergy, or those in the broader community who are not in relationship to God? Where is our customer? Who participates in our programmes? Who do they want to participate? Why do people come to us? It is quite fashionable for churches and seminaries to pride themselves on not being 'market driven', claiming that they are focused on being 'faithful' rather than 'successful'. That is fine if it is not simply a cover-up for the reality that we are in fact being driven by a different market (in schools, the faculty; in churches, the pastoral staff or a core of the congregation). It is wrong if we are using faithfulness as an excuse to keep on doing what we want to do rather than critically examining everything in terms of the mission.

What are the unique strengths of this organization? What special resources do we have? Why us? How do we differ from other organizations like us? Is how we do what we do unique and integral to our mission? What are our limits?

What would be lost if we ceased to exist? If we went out of business today, who would miss us? How would our 'customers' be served? These are some of the questions that a good mission statement might address.

The mission statement might also include theological distinctives, ethnic or cultural distinctives, organizational beliefs or values (although I will argue for a separate statement here) and any philosophy or character traits of importance.

There is no single 'correct' form for a mission statement. There is not one model. They are tools for the organization. They should take a form that works for your organization. What you want is a document that sets out the mission you believe in, that your leadership team owns, that your members want to carry out, and that your constituencies understand and support.

We must understand who we are before we can evaluate what we are doing. It is an issue of stewardship and accountability. Do you have a vision for your organization that gives you hope, that compels you into tomorrow? Are you articulating that vision in everything that you do? Are you offering hope to your people? When speaking at Regent College I usually underline both our mission to provide theological education to the whole people of God, and the reality that God is visibly at work in our midst transforming the lives of students.

Focusing on the vision keeps us asking critical questions about who we are. We do not want simply to maintain what we have always done. Take the church for example. What does the church need to be to point the men and women of the 21st century to God? Recent research on the Canadian church indicates that 60% of Canadians believe in God, in Christ, in the resurrection and the Bible. Yet only 2% to 4% have anything to do with the existing church. Perhaps we need a new vision for the Canadian church, with new models to equip the 56% 'non-church' Christians to live for Christ in this world.

Vision keeps asking questions of renewal! This is what leadership is all about. It is about getting yourself and your people excited about what God will do through you in the years ahead.

What is important to us? (Strategic planning)

The second question in our ten steps to the vision focuses our attention on a much-neglected aspect of the planning process – the role of organizational culture in shaping the life and future of the organization. I want to develop a response to this question in detail in the next chapter when I look at influencing with values. For now, let me note in summary that every organization has a hidden set of cultural assumptions that reflect the true beliefs of the organization and are manifested in the behaviours of the organization. They may or may not be expressed in the organization's official statement of values. One of the most important roles of the leader is to teach, model and reinforce a stated set of values in such a way that they become the shared values of the organization and are embedded in the organizational culture. These values wedded with the mission give body and soul to the vision we offer. This is an area of personal passion for me. We will come back to it.

Where in the world are we? (Strategic planning)

This is the research question. It is often called the situational analysis. It is the point when the planning process brings every aspect of the organization under the spotlight of the mission and the values of the organization and assesses the organization's strengths and weaknesses, its opportunities and challenges. In answering this question, the organization usually conducts an environmental or external audit as well as an organizational or internal audit.

1. The environmental audit
In the environmental audit, we look at *social trends and demographic information* that might be important to the implementation of our strategies. What is going on in the world today? What has changed since we last reviewed our situation? How might things be different in the next decade? How might changes in our environment affect us? We look closely at those we seek to serve, our clients or 'customers'.

What are they 'buying'? What could cause this to change? Why do they participate in our programmes? What is the exchange? When do they participate? How do they make decisions to participate? Where do they participate? How do they perceive us? Similarly we look at our primary sources of support and ask the same questions.

This is a time to list all other publics or constituencies whose attitudes and behaviours have an impact on the implementation of our strategies. Which publics are most influential? Why do they have an impact on the organization? What are their objectives and the reasons for their concern with our organization? What could cause this to change? How do they perceive us?

The environmental audit also looks at competitors. We do not like to use this language in Christian circles, but I am talking about all other organizations which are providing similar services for our intended 'customers' or participants. Who are our major competitors? How do they compete? What are their strengths and weaknesses?

And finally, this part of the audit looks also at the way changing technologies might affect the mission of the organization, the needs that the organization addresses, the services that the organization offers and the strategies used by the organization.

2. The organizational audit
The organizational or internal audit focuses on *programmes and services*. Every programme, service and activity of the organization should be listed. How central is this activity to the organizational mission? Will the need being addressed by this activity still be significant in five years? Is the level at which the need is being met a good return on the organization's investment of its resources? Similarly with the organizational audit, every department and, ideally, every position in the organization, is reviewed in terms of its contribution to the mission and the values. Is this a good return for the mission that calls us together?

Out of these two audits, the leadership and planning team identify the critical issues that must be addressed by the organization as it moves into its future. They may be issues of direction, of resources, of personnel, of facilities. They are identified, often with alternatives, as issues that must be included in the ongoing planning effort.

The environmental and organizational audits are often the most time-consuming aspects of the planning process. But they are important. They keep us from letting planning become simply an uncritical extension of the present into the future. And they provide the backdrop of reality for the vision. For a vision to offer hope it must emerge realistically from the situation in which we find ourselves today. Only then can it transcend the present and point us to tomorrow.

Where do we want to be? (Strategic planning)

With this stage of the planning process, the vision begins to take shape. This is the fun part. Using a management tool called a scenario, a vision is drafted and debated. After a brief look at the rest of the ten steps, I will return to the development of the scenario, the vision statement, in the rest of this chapter. It is a vision of a future that excites you, a future in which the mission and the values of your church or organization are being lived out with excellence, a future that addresses the needs and concerns of today and sees a difference being made by your organization.

What can we do? (Operational planning)

With the creation and organizational ownership of the scenario or vision, the strategic planning process is completed. Here I would argue that the leadership team should take over and translate that vision into an organizational plan for the next five years.

The first question that the leadership team wrestles with is: Given this vision of our future, what can we actually do in the next five years? At this point the leadership team sits down and balances the goals of the scenario and the critical issues of the audit with the reality of fiscal and physical projections and makes decisions about what will in fact be done over the next five years to move us towards that scenario, to address those issues.

At Regent College we call this the Five Year Financial Plan. We project a realistic budget alongside the strategies we would like to develop for the short term, allowing the vision of the strategies to stretch the budget and letting the constraints of the budget speak realism to the selection of strategies. This is the decision point. This is another responsibility that leaders are paid for. Here the hard decisions are made to determine exactly what we can accomplish over each of the next five years to keep us moving towards the shared vision of the future with fiscal responsibility.

How should we do it (Operational planning)

Drawing up the Five Year Financial Plan results in a selected set of strategies, unified goals, objectives and actions that we want to shape the way we live out our mission and values each of the next few years. For example, at Regent in support of our missional commitment to equip the laity, we may select a specific strategy for implementation next year. Selecting a strategy has financial ramifications. It may mean we must postpone other strategies for a few years. This is the kind of decision that is made at this leadership decision point.

When will we do it? (Operational planning)

At the decision point, selected strategies are identified for the time frame of the Five Year Financial Plan. These strategies should be defined in terms of key objectives for each year, forming the annual plan that finds its quantitative expression in the annual budget.

You have probably read a dozen definitions of objectives, but let me repeat the definition one more time. Objectives are stated levels of performance or effectiveness representing realistic steps towards fulfilling the mission and values of the organization. They should be specific results-oriented statements. Their accomplishment should be measurable so that we can know when they have been attained. Finally, objectives should be connected to the reward system. Recognition (thanks) or rewards should be directly related to the successful completion of the assigned objectives because the key objectives establish the time line that keeps the process moving strategically in line with the scenario – the shared vision.

Who will get us there? (Operational planning)

Delegation. Most plans fail precisely at this point. We do not have a working plan until each objective has been owned by someone who accepts responsibility to see that it is initiated and completed. This person assumes ownership of the results identified by the objective and has flexibility to modify the actions that are needed to produce those results. This is delegation. It is the point at which the plan moves from a shared vision to owned actions.

How are we doing? (Review and evaluation)

Accountability. The ninth step to the vision is actually review and evaluation. It is the feedback loop that tells us whether or not the actions of organization are in fact moving us towards our vision. The feedback comes through two loops. Information on the progress and effectiveness of the strategies returns to the leadership team and is taken into account in the operational planning when we decide what we can do for the next five years. The missional implications of the feedback – are we in fact fulfilling our mission by using these strategies? – is taken into account by the planning leadership in the strategic planning, when we look again at the mission, where we are, and where we want to be.

Was God pleased? (Review and evaluation)

The final question is ultimate and strategic. It, too, is evaluative and brings us back to our vision – to our mission and values. Are we fulfilling the mission to which God has called us? Are we doing it in a manner that reflects our value commitments before God? Has our living out of our vision pointed people to God? Have they seen the presence of Christ in our midst?

Our planning processes can be effective and keep our organizations and churches alive and active. But if our vision is not inspired by God, if our values are not shaped by the presence of Christ, if our strategies do not point people to God, then we have failed and probably should go out of business. Planning is a way to bring vision to reality. It is a way to involve others in a shared vision. It is also a time to listen to God, to see what God is doing in our midst and to allow our vision to be shaped by his Spirit.

The Scenario: A Vision for Hope

As I noted earlier, the vision statement or scenario is a picture of what our organization might look like if the mission and values are incarnated in the future. This is the part of the planning process that is fun. It is also one of the most important components. I tend to think of it as the highlight of the planning process. Given the mission, history, values, resources and environment of our organization, this is where the future is created, where change can take place.

A scenario is a narrative picture of your community or organization in the future. It is a presentation of one way your future could look. A scenario is an understandable and positive description of your future, including ministries, programmes, services and products in place and the results of these activities. It is a planning tool designed to clarify options for the future and move the organization or community towards consensus and ownership of that future. A scenario is a statement of faith – a vision of how we see God working in our tomorrow.

When the planning team or leadership has reviewed and committed itself to the mission, affirmed its basic cultural assumptions and institutional values, assessed the strengths and weaknesses of its internal resources, evaluated critically its external environment including the trends impacting its ministry, and identified the critical issues needing resolution, then this information needs to be translated into some pictures of the future. These pictures or scenarios assist the planning committee and leadership in selecting the directions (goals) we want to pursue given the constraints of the mission, values, resources and environment.

What is the purpose of a scenario?

Why take the time to construct a scenario? There are five reasons:

1. Scenarios clarify directions for the organization
They help the decision makers see more clearly what their choices are. They feature the results of decisions that are being made today.

2. Scenarios become the basis of goals for organizational energies
Once a scenario or vision statement has been adopted and owned as a direction towards which the community is committed, it is translated into goals and objectives to allocate the organization's resources and energies. If Regent College's vision for the 21st century is to be an international graduate school serving the Pacific Rim, that direction will channel funding and energy away from increasing our involvement in Europe and Africa, and towards expanded service and programmes in Asia.

3. Scenarios are excellent tools for communication, motivation and consensus building
It is much easier to get excited about a good scenario than about a list of goals and objectives. The goals and objectives set out in our planning end up on shelves, except for their important role in the control functions of leadership. Yet the scenarios, the statements of vision that capture the imagination and stir the spirit, continue to be vital living documents communicating our vision clearly to people inside and outside our organization. The scenario lets people know

where we are going. Because it communicates enthusiasm it motivates people within the organization to move on to implementation and it encourages people outside to provide the support and to participate in the programmes and services. Again, it is easier to build a consensus around an exciting vision than around specific goals and objectives.

4. Scenarios can prevent uncritical extension of present trends
Peter Drucker points out that it is all too easy for planners to write goals that simply extend current trends. He argues that leaders must avoid allocating resources to the defence of yesterday.[29] Scenarios can leapfrog over present trends into the future and raise necessary questions about the long-range validity of some trends.

5. Scenarios make change easier to introduce
Because they are looking 'into the distance', they are safe, non-threatening. People can deal with the issues raised 'academically', theoretically, without feeling the pain of change now. I like to focus my scenarios ten to fifteen years in the future. That way people who might worry about a proposed change if they thought it would affect them today will not be threatened by something that will happen after they are gone! Fifteen years from now is not too threatening to most people, and they can talk dispassionately about the issues involved. Interestingly, once they have taken ownership for the vision 'out there', they will start to make things happen immediately. It changes one's perspective.

One year I served as the planning consultant to the West Coast region of a US denomination. We used this scenario technique and people who usually avoided planning meetings began to get excited. They started to talk about things that up to that point had been taboo. Each board and committee developed and shared scenarios and the combined leadership began to get excited about the future and the ways they could work together to make that future happen. If you can get people talking about results in the future, they become much less defensive of strategies in the present.

Who presents scenarios?

Who writes vision statements? It really depends on the organization and its current situation. It could be only the president or the pastor. It could include all members of the leadership team. It could be extended to the chairs of individual boards or departments. At Regent College I like all of our cabinet officers to present scenarios to the planning committee, picturing their vision for the future of Regent through the eyes of their departments. From their combined vision, I prepare a college-wide scenario that is also debated and discussed by the committee, the faculty and the board. My approach is shaped strongly by Peter Block, who in *The Empowered Manager* argues that every manager within any organization should be regularly drafting a vision statement – a statement of how their piece of the organization might perform with excellence. Block notes that every manager is working from some vision anyway. The leader's job is to elicit that vision and allow it to contribute to the organization's vision of tomorrow.[30]

In one church I attended, the vision statement was normally drafted initially by the pastor and then modified from the various levels of discussion. As I noted earlier, when I worked with the denominational group, each board developed its scenario with one member assigned to write it and present it to the combined boards.

It is important that everyone whom we want to own the outcome of the planning process feels that they are represented in the scenarios. They do not all need a chance to develop a scenario and present it, but they all need to know that they have been heard and that they still fit in the picture of the future.

Personally, I believe this is the most renewing part of the leadership task. It is the opportunity to look ahead and project how God might use you and your organization over the next decade. The more I write and share scenarios for Regent, the more excited I get about the future of Regent. Which brings me to an important point for leaders. *If you cannot get enthusiastic about a scenario for the future of your church or organization, maybe it is time to change jobs!* This is a time to test your faith, your vision. When you look at the needs that your organization addresses, when you review its mission and values, are you compelled to live out those values in your life and work? Does that mission still draw you to invest your life and energy? Can you envision a picture of your organization ten years from now making such a difference in this world that you want to be part of making it happen? It is difficult to lead others if we are not led by our vision of what God wants to accomplish through us.

To whom are scenarios presented?

Again, this depends on the organizational structure. On a managerial scale, I would like all of our managers to have a scenario in mind if not on paper. I would expect this of all members of a church staff as well. Scenarios can be presented to the board, to the congregation, or to a strategic planning committee. Normally the strategic planning committee is the sounding board for the initial scenarios. My preference is to have the key leadership people of the organization prepare a 10- to 15- minute scenario and share it with the committee. Out of that discussion, someone should be assigned the responsibility of drafting an organization-wide scenario which will be presented, discussed and modified until ownership is achieved. This takes time, but it is fun and it is important. Once a future is owned, the rest of the planning process falls into line. Everything else is simply looking for the most effective and efficient strategies to bring that future about.

But remember, a scenario is a faith statement; it is not an absolute statement of future reality. We prepare scenarios together, in community, but always on our knees before God. The process is important and can lead to important decisions for our organization. But the process, the scenario, the plan do not necessarily declare the will of God. Leaders do their best to draw the wisest scenario out of the community that they lead, understanding that it is God's plan with which they are seeking to align their organization's resources and energies.

What makes a good scenario?

I have found eight elements to be important in creating a good scenario:

1. The scenario should articulate the mission and values
Any statement of vision for an organization should be a reinforcement and articulation of the existing mission and value commitments – unless the scenario is being used explicitly to change the mission.

2. The scenario should sketch a picture of what the future will look like
At this stage do not worry about how to get there, the strategies and resources. Work for the ideal as you see it completed ten to fifteen years from now. Sometimes this takes a little leadership effort because institutions have a tendency to want to talk about today's strategies rather than tomorrow's results. A good scenario, however, will keep focused on the future.

3. The scenario should look ten to fifteen years ahead
This is far enough in the future not to be an immediate threat of change. As I noted above, everyone can talk comfortably about the far-off future. But if we start threatening what is being done today, the scenario will be resisted. Ten to fifteen years off keeps discussion at the level of theory and principles and avoids the personalized affective dimension. Your scenario needs to be far enough in the future for people to feel safe.

4. The scenario should be anchored in the present
It cannot be unrealistic. It needs to be a logical future given what we know about today and who we are. A good scenario will also not be destructive of anyone's future. Again, if the future attacks the present too strongly, it will be resisted. It must not challenge the present, but rather hold up an exciting future that can be owned without having to sacrifice people's beliefs today. You can stretch people's thinking with

a scenario, but it will be shot down if it attacks their strongly held personal commitments today.

I ran into this during one of Regent's planning processes. I presented a scenario for the future that emphasized a picture of Regent as a network of interrelated learning communities around the world. While the scenario attempted to affirm the present commitments to the Vancouver campus, it showed the most exciting developments and growth off campus. Unfortunately, a large segment of the planning committee had committed themselves primarily to the campus programme. They read into the scenario a destruction of the Vancouver programme for the sake of extended programming. This was not my intent but it was, in fact, the way the scenario was heard and read. Consequently it was not approved and I had to prepare a revised scenario to underline my continued commitment to the Vancouver campus programming for the laity.

5. The scenario should have a dream side
It should have a faith component that stretches people's thinking. What might God do with your church or organization? What would we really like to do to fulfil our mission, even if it seems just out of reach? Sometimes the visualization of a scenario can in fact generate the resources or opportunities that make that dream happen. If the planning process is appropriately integrated with prayer, the scenario may include a vision of what we think God wants us to be, even though we do not now see how it would be possible. A good scenario is practical and realistic and a risk taken in faith.

6. The scenario should include results as well as programmes
I have been alluding to this all along. Do not just say you will provide a programme to feed the homeless. Tell how many homeless people will be fed and housed and what has happened to those you have already served. What difference will your programme make in their lives? It is too easy for us to describe our future in terms of programmes, services and staffing. A scenario is much more exciting when it talks in terms of impact and results. What difference will your

church or organization be making in your community, with your constituencies, in 2010? It is that difference that captures people's imagination, not your programmes.

7. *The scenario should be flexible*
Even as it stretches, it should be feasible, integrating faith and realism. It also, however, needs to have room for adjusting to new realities. Scenarios are never fixed, never set in concrete. They must always be open to change as new information surfaces. In a rapidly changing world, our pictures of a decade ahead are tenuous at best. Scenarios are always open to discussion and modification. They are tools to open discussion about the future. They are not the future.

8. *The scenario should describe a future you could own!*
It should generate enthusiasm in you and everyone with whom you share it. It should be exciting, rallying, something you want to get behind. The scenario or vision statement takes the mission and values of your church or organization and creates an energizing picture of the future that compels you and your people to want to work towards it. Try it: Pretend you are a reporter for the local paper or magazine and that you are currently looking at your organization on a particular day in 2010. Describe what you see: The programmes in place, the people involved, the impact the programmes and services have. Can you get energized by the vision?

For several years I taught a strategic planning seminar. On the Friday of the week-long intensive course, each participant would present a very brief seven-minute version of a scenario for their church or organization to the class. It was the highlight of the week. People would get excited and their excitement would be communicated through the room. Leaders would find renewal in a renewed vision as they shared that vision with others. It was a very emotional time. The scenario is a powerful tool for leadership.

Articulating the vision is one of the primary responsibilities of leadership. Servant leaders, in relationship with those for whom they are responsible, lift up a possible vision of

God's future – a future in which we want to participate. This shared vision controls our leadership and motivates our people as they own it and it becomes theirs.

Conclusion: A Compelling Vision

To end this section on empowering vision, it is appropriate to read a vision statement written by the apostle John:

> Then I saw a new heaven and a new earth, for the first heaven and the first earth had vanished, and there was no longer any sea. I saw the holy city, new Jerusalem, coming down out of heaven from God, made ready like a bride adorned for her husband. I heard a loud voice proclaiming from the throne: 'Now at last God has his dwelling among (men and women)! He will dwell among them and they shall be his people, and God himself will be with them. He will wipe every tear from their eyes; there shall be an end to death, and to mourning and crying and pain; for the old order has passed away!'...
>
> I saw no temple in the city; for its temple was the sovereign Lord God and the Lamb. And the city had no need of sun or moon to shine upon it; for the glory of God gave it light, and its lamp was the Lamb. By its light shall the nations walk, and the kings of the earth shall bring into it all their splendour. The gates of the city shall never be shut by day – and there will be no night. The wealth and splendour of the nations shall be brought into it; but nothing unclean shall ever enter, nor anyone whose ways are false or foul, but only those who are inscribed in the Lamb's roll of the living.
>
> Then he showed me the river of the water of life, sparkling like crystal, flowing from the throne of God and of the Lamb down the middle of the city's street. On either side of the river stood a tree of life, which yields twelve crops of fruit, one for each month of the year. The leaves of the trees serve for the healing of nations, and every accursed thing shall disappear. The throne of God and of the Lamb will be there, and his servants shall worship him; they shall see him face to face, and bear his name on their foreheads. There shall be no more night,

nor will they need the light of lamp or sun, for the lord God will give them light; and they shall reign for evermore . (Rev. 21:1–4, 22–27; 22:1–5)[31]

Now that is a vision to follow!

Notes

[1] See N.T. Wright, *The Epistles of Paul to the Colossians and to Philemon: An Introduction and Commentary*, Tyndale New Testament Commentaries, vol. 12 (Grand Rapids: Eerdmans, 1988), for this alternative translation of verse 6 of Philemon.

[2] Max DePree, *Leadership is an Art* (East Lansing: Michigan State University Press, 1987), 61.

[3] Max DePree, *Leadership Jazz* (New York: Doubleday, 1992), 82.

[4] DePree, *Leadership is an Art*, 11.

[5] DePree, *Leadership is an Art*, 82–83.

[6] Charles Handy, *The Age of Unreason* (Boston: Harvard Business School Press, 1989); *The Age of Paradox* (Boston: Harvard Business School Press, 1994).

[7] Handy, *Age of Unreason*, 5–9.

[8] See Stan Davis and Christopher Meyer, *Blur: The Speed of Change in a Connected Economy* (Reading, Mass.: Addison-Wesley, 1998), 13.

[9] Russell Chandler, *Racing Toward 2001* (Grand Rapids: Zondervan, 1992), 314.

[10] Faith Popcorn, *The Popcorn Report* (New York: Doubleday, 1991), 41.

[11] Davis and Meyer, *Blur*, 167.

[12] Handy, *Age of Unreason*, 184.

[13] Bill Breen, 'Money Isn't Everything', *Fast Company* (April–May 1998), 240.

[14] Esther Dyson, *Release 2.0: A Design for Living in the Digital Age* (New York: Broadway Books, 1997), 77.

[15] Stephen R. Covey, 'Servant-Leadership from the Inside Out', *Insights on Leadership*, xiv.

[16] Davis and Meyer, *Blur*, 217–218.

[17] Comments made at a seminar.

[18] Davis and Meyer, *Blur*, 13.

[19] Davis and Meyer, *Blur*, 148, 198, 201.

[20] Peter F. Drucker, *Post-Capitalist Society* (New York: Harper-Business, 1993), 42; see also Dyson, *Release*, 81.

[21] Handy, *Age of Unreason*, 184.

[22] Tom Peters, *The Circle of Innovation* (New York: Knopf, 1997), 395–423.

[23] Jeremy Rifkin, *The End of Work* (New York: Putnam, 1995), 238–239.

[24] Eugene Linden, *The Future in Plain Sight* (New York: Simon & Schuster, 1998), 79.

[25] Darrell L. Guder, *Missional Church* (Grand Rapids: Eerdmans, 1998), 1.

[26] Guder, *Church*, 44.

[27] Jürgen Moltmann, *Hope and Planning* (New York: Harper & Row, 1971), 184–190; see also Ray S. Anderson, *Minding God's Business* (Grand Rapids: Eerdmans, 1986), 139–140.

[28] Edgar H. Schein, *Organizational Culture and Leadership* (San Francisco: Jossey-Bass, 1992^2), 53.

[29] Peter F. Drucker, *Managing in Turbulent Times* (New York: Harper & Row, 1980), 45.

[30] Block, *Manager*, 107, 123.

[31] New English Bible translation.

Chapter IV

Influencing with Values

Fruit: Character and Values

Again we turn to our guide, Jude, to set our direction. 'Autumn trees without fruit and uprooted, twice dead.' As we noted in chapter one, trees without roots produce no fruit. The leaders that Jude is opposing have nothing to offer the people of his community. They have no character, no credibility, and consequently they have no values worth embedding in the culture of their community. Their leadership is not rooted in the love of God for his people. They love only themselves. They are doubly useless – not grounded in a relationship empowered by God and, therefore, not producing any growth in their community.

The biblical leader reveals a character shaped in relationship to God that spills over into all relationships. Such leaders live and model the kind of values that they would like to see expressed in the way the organization or community conducts its corporate life.

Leadership with character produces value-laden fruit. Leaders who find their identity in their relationship with God nurture organizations that care for people as persons loved by God. Leaders who find their security in their walk with Christ will nourish communities where diversity is comfortably embraced and where wounded relationships are reconciled and healed. Leaders

> Leadership is a relationship of trust where commitments flow from character.

who place their hope in God will be people who respect commitments, who keep promises, who encourage trust.

In his recent book *Mr. Ives' Christmas*[1] Pulitzer Prize-winning author Oscar Hijuelos introduces us to Ives, a deeply spiritual man, who, despite his beginnings in an orphanage, has made an enviable life for himself. A successful Madison Avenue advertising illustrator, Ives is married to a vivacious, artistic woman, Annie, who shares his aesthetic passions and strong beliefs. They live in New York City, where they raise their children, Robert and Caroline, with remarkable fair-mindedness and moral judgement. He rises to a vice-presidency at the advertising agency and lives comfortably with a community of friends. Robert will be entering seminary after high school to prepare for ordination as a priest in the Catholic Church.

But Ives' perfect world is shattered when his seventeen-year-old son Robert is gunned down by a teenage mugger at Christmas. Ives is overwhelmed by grief and struggles with doubts about the very values that have shaped his life and faith.

The novel follows Ives through the next 25 years of his life as he searches for peace and understanding. In the end, his personal integrity, his character, the values and faith that he taught to his children, compel him to reconcile with and forgive his son's murderer. Only then can he return to the core of who he is and re-engage the life around him. To his friends he is a man of character – a person who navigates his life and work with deeply held values that shape his behaviour and influence the lives of those around him. Ives' leadership at work and living at home were constrained and empowered by his character and commitments, his faith and values.

Who are you? And who cares? Leadership flows from character, from who you are. And leaders add value to all of the relationships in which they are engaged; that is why people care about leadership. Leadership is about adding value to an organization and its people out of the strength of the character and values of the leader – character and values rooted in the love of God.

The Colossian Church: A Community of Character

Now, let's turn again to our Colossian community and see what values shape their life together. This time imagine yourself in a meeting of the Colossian church shortly after Tychicus and Onesimus arrived with Paul's letters to Philemon and to the Colossians. The church has assembled in the home of one of the elders. People are sitting around, some on chairs, some on the floor, some standing. A new letter has been received from Paul writing from prison.

In a day without Bibles, this is a major event. The letter is to be read today and a word from God is going to be received through the apostle Paul. There is an air of excitement and anticipation throughout the congregation. But there is also a ripple of anxiety and discomfort. You can feel the tension. Sitting in the room are Philemon and Onesimus. Philemon, one of the leaders of this church, was betrayed last year by one of his family slaves who stole from him and ran away. Philemon had been very upset about the experience and had shared it with the congregation.

And now, here sits Onesimus, the runaway slave – sent back as a believer by Paul himself. We know that Philemon also received a personal letter from Paul – that must account for his willingness to have Onesimus here in the same room with him. Perhaps he will share Paul's letter with us.

How are we supposed to deal with this? Onesimus is a slave! Should he be here? Yet he seems to be a genuinely converted believer – and he has Paul's blessing. Should we let Christian slaves into our church? What about his crime? He stole from Philemon and ran away. That is punishable by death. Do we ignore that? Apparently Paul wants Philemon to take Onesimus back into his house, reinstate him as a member of his staff, and accept him as a Christian brother.

What's our role in this? We are the Christian community in Colosse. We are supposed to be the body of Christ. We know that Philemon is an important and active member of this community. And now we need to embrace Onesimus. How do we do this? How do we deal with the conflict that is obviously going on in many minds in this room? Can this really be of God if it is causing all this conflict for us?

It's not hard to imagine this scene on the Sunday after Tychicus and Onesimus arrived. Put yourself in their place and listen to parts of the letter to the Colossians, keeping in mind that Philemon and Onesimus are sitting here listening as well.

So then, just as you received Christ Jesus as Lord, continue to live in him, rooted and built up in him, strengthened in the faith as you were taught, and overflowing with thankfulness ...

Since ... you have been raised with Christ, set your hearts on things above, where Christ is seated at the right hand of God. Set your minds on things above, not on earthly things. For you died, and your life is now hidden with Christ in God. When Christ, who is your life, appears, then you also will appear with him in glory.

Put to death, therefore, whatever belongs to your earthly nature: sexual immorality, impurity, lust, evil desires and greed, which is idolatry. Because of these, the wrath of God is coming. You used to walk in these ways, in the life you once lived. But now you must rid yourselves of all such things as these: anger, rage, malice, slander and filthy language from your lips. Do not lie to each other, since you have taken off your old self with its practices and have put on the new self which is being renewed in knowledge in the image of its Creator. Here there is no Greek or Jew, circumcised or uncircumcised, barbarian, Scythian, slave or free, but Christ is all, and is in all.

Therefore, as God's chosen people, holy and dearly loved, clothe yourselves with compassion, kindness, humility, gentleness and patience. Bear with each other and forgive whatever grievances you may have against one another. Forgive as the Lord forgave you. And over all these virtues put on love, which binds them all together in perfect unity.

Let the peace of Christ rule in your hearts, since as members of one body you were called to peace. And be thankful. Let the word of Christ dwell in you richly as you teach and admonish one another with all wisdom, and as you sing psalms, hymns and spiritual songs with gratitude in your hearts to God. And whatever you do, whether in word or deed, do it all in the name of the Lord Jesus, giving thanks to God the Father through him.

Wives, submit to your husbands, as is fitting in the Lord. Husbands, love your wives and do not be harsh with them.

Children, obey your parents in everything, for this pleases the Lord. Fathers, do not embitter your children, or they will become discouraged.

Slaves obey your earthly masters in everything; and do it not only when their eye is on you and to win their favour, but with sincerity of heart and reverence for the Lord. Whatever you do, work at it with all your heart, as working for the Lord, not for human masters, since you know that you will receive an inheritance from the Lord as a reward. It is the Lord Christ you are serving. Those who do wrong will be repaid for their wrongs, and there is no favouritism.

Masters, provide your slaves with what is right and fair, because you know that you also have a Master in heaven. (Col. 2:6–7; 3:1 – 4:1)

Powerful words for a church struggling with conflict. But what does this have to do with us nearly 2000 years later? Do we ever have conflict in our communities?!

For my personal recreation, I regularly participate in white-water canoe trips or mountain climbing. My friend Don and I have been roped together or shared a canoe now for nearly twenty-five years. We have grown close in this time, learned to trust each other and to care deeply about each other's lives.

Do we ever experience conflict? Only every time the canoe heads over rapids with me in the front! Don and I are both opinionated, controlling people with very definite ideas how to get through the water and rocks alive. However, I sit in the front. I am the first to taste the rapids, and when my paddle goes into the water, I have a major effect on the control of the canoe whether Don agrees or not. Don and I have debated procedures before, during and after successful runs and total disasters. We have experienced many conflicts. But we care for each other and have linked our survival by roping up on a mountain or sharing a canoe on the river. We both have a vested interest in the best outcome and are willing to confront each other on our behaviours and procedures and listen to the other person carefully. Failure to listen usually ends up with one or both of us swimming downstream! Close community includes conflict. But caring relationships work for the resolution of conflict and the growth of community.

I would like to reflect on conflict, confrontation, character and accountability, and see if we can learn something about values from the way Paul approached this situation in Colosse.

Should there be conflict in a Christian community?

What is conflict? Conflict, as the psychologists tell us, is not something that happens between two people. It is something that happens in us as individuals when we encounter differences, something that does not fit our understanding of a situation.

Conflict is probably a required corollary of community. The very definition of Christian community includes an acceptance of diversity – witness Philemon and Onesimus – and diversity means differences: differences of approach, of values, of perspective, of opinions, of expectations, of hopes, of commitments. And difference causes conflict.

Conflict is not only possible in Christian community, it may be a necessary by-product of community that is an important catalyst for growth as we learn to adjust to the differences caused by the diversity of community. No conflict may suggest no diversity and possibly no growth. Both Philemon and Onesimus experienced conflict before and during their reconciliation and their presence probably produced conflict in many of the members of the Colossian church. On this side of heaven, I believe there will always be conflict in Christian community as we struggle to learn to live like the body of Christ in this world. And it is precisely this conflict that produces character.

If conflict is inevitable, how do we handle it?

Here I think Paul gives us a good model; a model I would call caring confrontation and accountability over against criticism and gossip. In the passage we read, he discards anger, rage, malice and slander as appropriate characteristics for a Christian community. He affirms compassion, kindness, humility, gentleness, patience, forgiveness and love as the marks of Christian character. It is clear that Paul sees a caring attitude of love dominating all community relationships. Yet he goes on to encourage the Colossians to engage one another in teaching and instruction or confrontation that emerges from their study of God's word.

I believe Paul expects confrontation, but he expects it to be conducted in the context of a caring relationship, a relationship in which both parties are genuinely concerned about the growth and development of each other in the community. And as a leader that is exactly what he sets out to accomplish.

Let me distinguish between caring confrontation and criticism. I believe that confrontation addresses a person's behaviours or attitudes in light of that person's stated values or commitments, not my values or beliefs. Confrontation holds people accountable to live what they teach or claim to be important. It does not address their progress by standards that I hold up for myself. If confrontation is to be effective or constructive, there must be a caring relationship surrounding it. Within the context of a caring relationship you can hold me accountable to my own values and beliefs because I know you care and want to see me grow in my faith.

On the other hand, criticism attacks the other person without the supportive context of a caring relationship. Criticism may address a person's failure to live up to his or her commitments or beliefs but with little genuine interest in the person's growth and development. Often, however, criticism reflects my internal conflict. Because I am in conflict, I want you to change – not because I care about you, but because I am focusing on me. Criticism may be voiced to the person who is causing my conflict but is often directed to someone else about that person. This I call gossip.

Caring confrontation is concerned about the other person's growth and emerges within a relationship of trust. Criticism emerges from our own conflict and usually destroys trust. Confrontation wants to see positive growth. Criticism wants to express hurt and conflict. Confrontation usually seeks resolution. Criticism usually seeks removal of my conflict.

In an organizational context, this distinction is important. Leaders are there to hold people accountable to the shared vision of the community and to the standards they have agreed to achieve. This happens in a caring relationship of influence. Leaders hold followers accountable to the shared vision, mission and values of the organization, *not* to the vision, values or opinions of the leader. Confrontation occurs in a relationship in which the leader cares about the follower and the vision they share. Confrontation measures progress against a shared organizational mission *owned by the follower*. Criticism usually occurs when the leader is self-focused and progress is measured by the leader's standards or mission.

I think this is the genius of Paul's confrontation with Philemon. Read his letter again and watch how Paul underlines his deep love for Philemon – the caring relationship – and holds Philemon accountable to act according to Philemon's commitments to a vision they share.

In the context of a deep and caring relationship, Paul has confronted Philemon with the implications of his commitments. Philemon is known for his encouragement of fellow believers and for his participation in and support of community, and this is what Paul appeals to. He does not attack the institution of slavery. He does not hold Philemon accountable for a value system that we in this century think he should have understood. Rather, he stays within the values and culture of Philemon and the Colossian church, but he lovingly points out to Philemon that his commitment to community might require him to take a second look at his relationship with Onesimus. I think we can learn five things about Paul's values and about the requirements for caring confrontation and accountability from the way he writes to Philemon.

1. A caring relationship
First, Paul clearly establishes the context of a caring relationship. There can be no question that Paul and Philemon are integrally bound by mutual respect and love.

2. Identification with the conflict of the other person
Paul brings Onesimus directly into that relationship by underlining his own deeply personal and spiritual relationship with the converted slave. Philemon can no longer deal with Onesimus as one who has offended him personally or as a subhuman slave. Now he must deal with his relationship with Paul. It is Paul that he must see when he looks at Onesimus.

3. Acceptance of the person's stated values and commitments as the starting point
Paul confronts Philemon with his own commitments. The opening prayer gives thanks for Philemon's contributions as a member of the Colossian community, his investment in the members of the church. The refreshment and encouragement for which Philemon is known, Paul now asks for himself and through him for Onesimus.

> Note that while there is strong expectation running throughout Paul's letter, there is no indication that the relationship with Philemon would be ended if Philemon doesn't comply. He resists using his authority, at least directly, and leaves it up to Philemon to decide how far he will go in his acceptance of Onesimus.

4. A personal investment in the resolution
Paul takes the cost of the confrontation on himself. He assumes Onesimus' debt and offers to cover all costs due to Philemon. Effective confrontation asks the question: What can I do to help you succeed in living up to your values? In this case Paul is willing to cover all of the debt that Onesimus owes Philemon.

5. A commitment to long-term accountability and growth
Paul builds accountability into the confrontation. He states that he will be visiting soon to see how things are going.

Philemon knows that the Paul who cares about him will be checking in to see how he has responded to his confrontation. Part of accountability is the willingness to have our progress monitored. People who care enough to confront you with your own values are marvellous friends to have. People who follow up and care enough to hold you accountable for your growth are wonderful gifts from God.

It is not hard to see the Christ-motif in Paul's approach. Two people are to be reconciled in Paul, who bears the cost of that reconciliation personally. Now there is a model for relational leadership – for servant leadership!

Conflict is inevitable in a Christian community. Yet conflict can be resolved through caring confrontation that invests itself in the growth and development of the other person. Confrontation and accountability, I believe, are values deeply embedded in the concept of community and must be embraced by leaders.

Leadership Is Being Oneself for Others

We have been looking at leadership as a relationship. Leadership is a relationship in which one person makes an investment in another to influence the behaviours, vision, values, beliefs or attitudes of the other person. This influence has two major purposes: the growth of the follower (and the leader) and the accomplishment of a mission or vision shared by both. As we saw above, the leadership relationship exists only when others choose to accept our influence and allow us to lead them.

Research by James Kouzes and Barry Posner has underlined the fact that people follow leaders who are credible, who have integrity, or what I would call character. By integrity or character they mean three things: personal values or beliefs, that is, a credo of what is right; capabilities or competence, that is, the ability to turn your words into actions; and trust or confidence in your ability to do what you believe.[2] Character is more than stated beliefs and values. Character is something that emerges from within; it comes from the soul. It

represents those deeply held beliefs or value commitments
that shape who you are, that control all that you do. I am
making a distinction here between character and stated
values. Stated values are the commitments that we affirm,
such as the Spirit-shaped characteristics we read about in
Colossians. Character, however, reflects those deeply held
beliefs out of which our behaviours and attitudes actually
emerge. If someone watches our actions, they will see our true
character, regardless of the values we espouse. Ideally, with
the help of the Spirit of God, our affirmations and our actions
will be consistent. That at least is our calling, I believe.

Kouzes and Posner argue that leadership starts with the
leader. It starts with a person of character, someone worth
following. Great leaders, Warren Bennis claims, are people
who are 'being themselves' with character and integrity.[3] You
do not become a great leader by seeking to be a leader. You
become an effective leader by living out of the strength of
your character, by living what you believe. That kind of character produces credibility, and people follow people who are
credible. We began this chapter with the accusation of Jude.
Lack of character is precisely Jude's concern. The would-be
leaders in his community had no roots. There was no God-
shaped character to give content to their leadership. They
were not believable as leaders. Leadership starts in the soul
with a desire to live out our calling in Christ as Spirit-shaped
people. Only in the strength of this relationship with God in
Christ are we in any position to offer leadership.

Six disciplines for maintaining credibility

In their book *Credibility* Kouzes and Posner outline six disciplines that leaders should work at continually to maintain
their integrity and credibility.[4] When it comes to building
character, none of these are substitutes for spending time
with God, but they are helpful reminders about important
components of the leadership relationship:

☞ **Discover yourself.** Take time to think through what you
    believe, looking at your life and actions to see what kind

of values are reflected by your behaviours and attitudes. What are the important value commitments that you bring to the table, that you want to model and are prepared to allow others to hold you to account for?

☛ **Appreciate your constituents.** Focus your attention on your people, understand them as they are. Value the diversity they represent and confront the conflict that emerges with differences. Kouzes and Posner want to shift the focus as quickly as possible from the self to others, so that trust can be built by listening to and caring about those for whom we are responsible.

☛ **Affirm *shared* values.** We will look at this in more detail below. Community is built upon shared vision and shared values. Leaders are responsible for articulating, modelling and reinforcing both vision and values in the life of the communities they seek to lead.

☛ **Develop capacity.** Make an investment in the followers that increases their ability to contribute. Following the model of Hersey and Blanchard that we looked at in Chapter 2, Kouzes and Posner want to see everyone growing into levels of maturity that allow them to lead out of deeply embedded values and compelling visions.

☛ **Serve a purpose.** For Kouzes and Posner, leadership is service. It focuses on the shared vision and empowers people to make a contribution to that vision. Again, the flow is from the character within outward in service of the vision and the people.

☛ **Sustain hope.** As people of vision and people of character, leaders keep hope alive. They have the courage to live out their vision and to strive to live out their values, and they encourage others to do the same. Character, in the final analysis, is based on a vision of God at work in this world and the renewing presence of the Spirit within us.

Character is life lived in relationship with God. It is about being the person whom God intends you to be for the sake of the people whom God brings across your path. People of character become leaders whether they hold a position of leadership or not. They are people whose integrity and credibility earn trust. People listen and follow. In the context of our Christian communities, we look for Christ-shaped character in our leaders, since leaders have a significant responsibility in shaping the character of our churches and organizations.

Character, Culture and Values

The first responsibility of leadership is to articulate the vision, to keep the mission and values before the church or organization. Effective leaders offer a compelling picture of the future that motivates people to get involved. The second responsibility of leadership, I believe, is to reinforce the culture. This is the point in our communities where the intersection of leadership and spirituality is most visible.

Character

The character of the community and the character of individual members of that community is what the leadership literature calls *organizational culture*. Current studies are repeatedly underlining the leader's responsibility for reinforcing the culture of the organization with intentional and personally held values.

This is an area of particular interest to me as I seek to bring my faith to bear on my leadership responsibilities. This is where I try to work out my own spirituality in the context of my positional responsibilities as a leader. I have a strong concern, almost a passion, about organizations being both effective and efficient and at the same time manifesting the fruit of the Spirit. I want to see organizations and churches run effectively and accountably with the best of leadership and stewardship. I also want to see them living out their corporate lives together in a way that reflects the presence of the Spirit of God in their midst. The fruit of the Spirit should be manifest in the way they do business together. I do not believe these are mutually exclusive. In fact, I believe that a Christian organization must by definition be both an effective organization and a vital Christian community. Now I do not know many places where this is true yet, which is why I prefer to avoid using the phrase 'Christian organization'. It is something we work on consciously and intentionally at Regent College, and we know that we still have a long way to go. But I believe strongly that we must keep working at it if we are to be leaders who reflect the presence of Christ in our communities.

Those of us in Christian leadership talk a lot about community, love, values and the fruit of the Spirit, and yet we frequently live and lead our organizations with actions that do not match our words. Max DePree, the friend and mentor that I have referred to, captures the link between actions and words very well in the story about his granddaughter told in his book *Leadership Jazz*:

> Esther, my wife, and I have a granddaughter named Zoe, the Greek word for 'life'. She was born prematurely and weighed one pound, seven ounces, so small that my wedding ring could slide up her arm to her shoulder. The neonatologist who first examined her told us that she had a 5 to 10 percent chance of living three days. When Esther and I scrubbed up for our first visit and saw Zoe in her isolette in the neonatal intensive care unit, she had two IVs in her navel, one in her foot, a monitor on each side of her chest, and a respirator tube and a feeding tube in her mouth.
>
> To complicate matters, Zoe's biological father had jumped ship the month before Zoe was born. Realizing this, a wise and caring nurse named Ruth gave me my instructions: 'For the next several months, at least, you're the surrogate father. I want you to come to the hospital every day to visit Zoe, and when you come, I would like you to rub her body and her legs and arms with the tip of your finger. While you're caressing her, you should tell her over and over how much you love her, because she has to be able to connect your voice to your touch.'
>
> Ruth was doing exactly the right thing on Zoe's behalf (and, of course, on my behalf as well), and without realizing it she was giving me one of the best possible descriptions of the work of a leader. At the

core of becoming a leader is the need always to connect one's voice and one's touch.[5]

Max DePree is calling us to practise what we preach, to live out our values in our organizational life, our community life together. He expects our character to be reflected in the way we lead within our organizations. Our behaviours are to be in sync with our sermons. Our voice should be seen in our touch.

Public television often has superb presentations about leadership. One series of *Classic Theater* focused on the story of the Borgias, Pope Alexander VI and his son Cesare Borgia, the Duke of the Romagna. If there was ever an example of the clash between stated values and personal character, the Borgias must be supreme. In the name of the Christian church and all the values it stands for, Rodrigo, Lucrezia and Cesare Borgia ruled with a self-serving wickedness that later became the model for Niccolo Machiavelli's *The Prince*, often seen as the prototypical description of an evil leader. They lied, cheated and used their power to play their friends and their enemies off against one another. They spoke the language of the holy church. Their actions were those of evil incarnate. Their true identity was not in their words but in their touch, in their behaviour.

Culture

When I am teaching leadership I often use a simple exercise with Tinkertoys. I break the class into small groups and give each group a can of Tinkertoys. They have 60 seconds to build the tallest possible self-standing structure, without talking. At the end of the 60 seconds, I measure each structure and we analyse why the groups did not perform better. Why are the structures so small and often disjointed? Most groups initially conclude that they did not have enough time. So we do the exercise again. Only this time, I give them three minutes to talk together and plan how to use their 60 seconds of Tinkertoy construction. After the planning time, I again ask for silence and the exercise is repeated with the same rules. This time, however, we have skyscrapers in the room! Nearly every group improves significantly when they have a plan for the use of their limited resources (time and supplies) and a role for each to play. Time is not the issue. Planning and delegation are key.

However, at the end of this second exercise, I usually ask the second- or third-place groups, 'If the objective was to have the tallest standing structure in the room, why didn't you knock down the other towers or take their materials?'

Most groups, particularly in Christian communities, are shocked at the suggestion and usually respond that it would not be right or fair or something like that, at which time I point out that they have a hidden value system or culture that is constraining their choice of strategies to achieve their objective. Their behaviour is being shaped by their values without any conscious awareness on their part.

This is a simplistic example, but it is exactly what is going on in all of our organizations and churches. Every organization has a hidden culture that has developed over the years that controls what is actually done regardless of the values we espouse. The problem is that when the stated values of the church or the organization are not in sync with the cultural beliefs and assumptions, it creates organizational dissonance and people get caught in the middle.

I believe that you can learn more about the culture of an organization by observing the behaviours and actions of the people than by reading the statement of organizational values. In organizations, people tend to live out the culture that they have been part of rather than the values that are articulated by the leadership. If we want to create community in our organizations or churches as an intentional value, we need to start with an understanding of the cultural values we are already reinforcing.

Over the last decade the importance of organizational culture, organizational value systems, has been emerging in the leadership literature. Books like *Corporate Cultures, In Search of Excellence, Creating Excellence, Passion for Excellence, Thriving on Chaos, Leadership Jazz, Credibility, Above the Bottom Line,* and *Leading Change*[6] have recognized that all organizations have deeply rooted beliefs and assumptions that shape the way those within the organizations live and work together, and that the relationship between the leader and the organization is a key variable in the reinforcement or change of these beliefs.

Edgar Schein, a distinguished professor at MIT's Sloan School of Management, goes so far as to suggest that perhaps the only thing of unique importance that leaders do is to create and manage culture.[7] In his excellent book *Organizational Culture and Leadership* Schein points out that our values are the observed manifestations of our organizational culture. He uses *values* here as the visible actions and publicly stated affirmations of what is important to us. Our actions are value statements as much as our affirmations. Hopefully they match. By *culture* Schein refers to the basic assumptions and beliefs that are shared by members of the organization and operate unconsciously,[8] defining the organization's view of itself. The elements of an organization's culture cannot be seen and are seldom talked about. But they are there as deeply and as powerfully at work as the beliefs that kept the class from knocking down the Tinkertoy towers.

Every organization has this hidden culture. It is formed out of the shared history and experiences of the organization as it develops and survives. The founding leadership of our churches and organizations implant the first seeds of the culture. Then, over time, the community living together develops some unconscious ways of doing things. 'The way things are done here' becomes automatic, reinforced over the years by what is valued and what is opposed. Tradition becomes strong and deeply rooted. Most of us can come up with illustrations easily from our church experience. Tradition is strong in churches and difficult to change. In North America most churches still meet at 11.00 on Sunday mornings to accommodate the milking of the cows – in spite of the fact that very few church members own cows anymore! And music! Every church has horror stories about the traditions involved in the music of the church. The organizational culture is that set of traditions, assumptions and beliefs that are taken for granted and operate unconsciously in all of our organizations.

Schein's research demonstrates that every organization has a hidden culture. Interestingly, he goes on to argue that most organizational cultures take shape around a similar pattern. The culture is formed as an unconscious institutional response to six basic issues: how the organization understands truth, time, space, human nature, human activity and human relationships.[9] Theological issues!

By *truth* he refers to the 'shared assumptions that define what is real and what is not ... how truth is ultimately to be determined, and whether truth is revealed or discovered'. By *time*, Schein is referring to the shared assumptions that define time, how time is measured, 'how many kinds of time there are, and the importance of time in the culture'. In terms of *space*, he sees organizations as having 'shared assumptions about space and its distribution, how space is allocated and owned, the symbolic meaning of space around the person', the role of space in defining intimacy, privacy or importance.[10]

His issues concerning *human nature, activity and relationships* touch the core of our work in the church and in theological education. They include the shared assumptions about what it means to be human. Is human nature good, evil or neutral? Are human beings perfectible or not? What is the right way for people to relate to their environment? What is the appropriate balance between activity or initiative and passivity and reaction? What is work? What is play? How are power and love distributed in human relationships? 'Is life cooperative or competitive; individualistic, group collaborative, or communal?'[11] How are conflicts resolved and decisions made?

Schein would argue that, without thinking about it, every organization forms assumptions about these six dimensions that become the context for all of its corporate life. These assumptions form a hidden pattern or worldview which he calls *culture*. That culture shapes the actions, decisions, policies and procedures of the organization in the formation of the values that govern all that the organization does.

Values

While we can work to learn about and understand the cultural assumptions operating in our organization, the role of leaders is targeted primarily at the values level. Here we work consciously to reinforce those values that we affirm by our every action and word. If the culture produces values that are not consistent with the affirmations we make, leaders must slowly and patiently continue to reinforce the stated values until they are embedded in the culture deep enough to last. The culture shapes the behaviours of the people in the organization. Leaders create and sustain culture in everything that they do. If we want to make a difference in our organizations, we need to be aware of this reality and be intentional with our actions, recognizing that we are working on cultural assumptions even as we articulate and implement vision. This may well be the place where leadership has the most significant long-range impact on the life and mission of the organization.

This brings us back to the discussion of planning. We focused above on the mission of the organization as critical to the leader's vision. What Schein underlines for us is the significance of the second question in our earlier planning model: What is important to us? I believe that a true vision includes both mission and values. It creates a picture of a future that captures who we are, both what we do and the values that we communicate in the doing of it. There are two systems involved in our organizational planning and leadership.

Let me illustrate with a simple story. Once I was visiting the office of a prestigious professor at a regional college, seeking to recruit him to teach in a continuing education programme. We were meeting in the evening since that was the only time available in both our schedules. During the discussion, the door of his office opened and a young student janitor came in with her vacuum cleaner. It was Thursday night and the professor's office was scheduled for cleaning. She proceeded to vacuum the floor, asking us to lift our feet when she needed to vacuum under our chairs. Finally, we had to stop talking because we could not hear anything over the roar of the vacuum cleaner. When she was finished, she left, we smiled and went on with the negotiations.

Now, was she doing her job? Yes and no. Yes, according to the purpose system of her objectives for the evening. No, according to the values system of what is important in the mission of her job. According to the traditional purpose system, she was doing precisely what she was supposed to do. Her piece of the organizational mission called for her to keep professors' offices clean, and her objective for Thursday night was to clean this professor's office. She was doing her job and progress could be measured against the mission, at least according to the purpose system.

However, the values system asks a different set of questions that also impact the mission. What are we about? What is important here? Under the values system, her job was not to keep the professor's office clean but to provide an environment that facilitated or made possible the professor's ministry. Her role was to support the professor's ministry and so further the mission of the organization. Had she been operating consciously under both systems she would have noted that the professor had a guest, recognized that the best support she could provide at that moment was *not* to clean the office, and then revised her own work schedule so she could do that office later.

Now, even in this illustration, we are dealing with assumed values. My critique of the janitor is based on my stated value that she is there to support the professor's ministry. On the other hand, she behaved differently, most likely acting out of the cultural values of her organization. She had already learned that she would be rewarded for cleaning this office on Thursdays, not for using her head and switching days. She was acting under a values system. However, her actions suggest that the governing value system preferred conformity to creativity.

There are two systems involved in the planning process. The purpose system (see the diagram below) is a pyramid of goals, objectives and actions descending from the organizational mission. The values system is a pyramid of values,

Two Systems of Strategic Planning

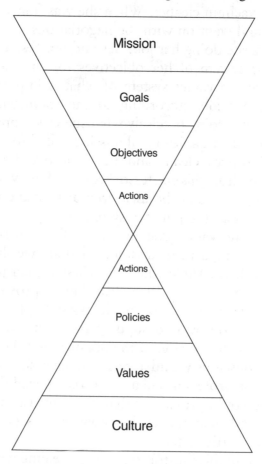

norms or policies, and actions ascending from the beliefs or culture of the organization. Both are important to the planning process of any organization. Both will impact the selection of strategies and the implementation of operational plans. Traditionally, planning has focused on the purpose system, setting goals and measurable objectives. Schein believes that it is absolutely essential that leaders examine the organizational culture and values system because culture constrains strategy.[12] It is difficult to plan beyond the boundaries of the culture, both the intentional value commitments and the unintentional unconscious culture or tradition that has developed over the organization's history.

When I was serving as a planning consultant to a US denomination, we had a classic example of the tension between the two systems. The denomination operated three campgrounds on the West Coast. Two of them barely broke even financially. One was so far in debt that the interest on the outstanding loans was greater than the property was worth! When I suggested that they consider selling one or more of the campgrounds, there was great resistance. It was too painful because the culture of the churches wanted to protect something that was important to them in their past. As one person said, 'But that's where my dad found the Lord!'

That is culture at work. Deep-seated beliefs and assumptions, traditions that control the way we do things – an affective response that was strong enough to hold fiscal reality at bay for years. It took some time for us to surface what was happening and bring the group to the realization that they were holding onto tradition and good feelings that in fact were hurting their ability to provide ministry today. They did sell off the campground eventually.

Organizational culture is a powerful force in all of our churches and organizations. It is a force that leaders must understand and address, because leaders create and reinforce organizational culture.

Leaders Create and Reinforce Culture

This whole area of organizational culture and leadership values has been an interest of mine for years. When I was completing my doctoral studies in New Testament, I financed my education by working as an administrator. I was painfully surprised to see very little crossover between these two arenas. Theologians who handled the Word of God all day would enter the halls of governance in the seminary with a style and behaviour that seemed rather different from the fruit of the Spirit I had been studying with them earlier. I do not want to single out any one school here. I find it true in Christian education everywhere. Nor is the church exempt.

Pastors often treat their staff and volunteers with a different set of values than they proclaim on Sunday morning. In the church the problem goes both ways. Business people who understand leadership and management and organizational culture will walk into a church board meeting and act as though they have left their brains at home. All of their experience and education is discarded as not being 'spiritual' enough for a good organizational decision at church.

By now you should realize that I do not agree with this dualism, this dichotomy between organization and community. When a group of men and women gather to accomplish a mission, by definition we are an organization. But we are more, much more. When we gather in the name of Christ, we are also a taste of the kingdom of God on earth. We are a community of the Spirit. We are a community whose organization is shaped both by its mission and by the gifting presence of the Spirit. I do not want to accept anything less than both effective organizational life and vital Christian community life. They are not mutually exclusive; they are essentially complementary. I realize that I am holding up an ideal – one that I cannot live up to. But I want to hold up a vision of what we should be, what, with God's help, we can be. At the very least, I want us to articulate how we think we should live and be prepared, like Philemon, to be held accountable for how we live up to our values and beliefs.

I think this principle holds true even for leaders who find themselves with leadership responsibilities in secular or corporate organizational settings. Relational leadership – servant leadership, leadership from character – is even more important when it is exercised in a community without the foundational assumptions of Christian faith. The leader is still the primary person to identify, reinforce and add the values that will shape the way the organization lives and does its business in the years ahead. This alone is sufficient reason for Christian men and women to seek leadership positions in our public and private corporations, locally and internationally. Leaders add value. Christian leaders, ideally, incarnate the biblical values articulated by Paul, with a strong commitment to respect for individuals and the interdependence of relationships. They know the value of community as a natural expression of human relationships grounded in the creative love of God. Christian leaders bring identity, hope and character to their leadership relationships. They have a wonderful opportunity – indeed the organization expects it of them – to add value to the organization in a way that communicates worth, purpose and hope, and that nurtures people's development and their growth in ability to participate in and contribute to the mission of the organization. Leadership is a relationship of character that shapes culture. Leaders have a responsibility to their organizational mission and to the people for whose development they are responsible.

When I am working with or in any organization it is normally the case that the organization has strongly stated values regarding the importance, care and development of its people. This is especially true of Christian communities. Yet many 'Christian' organizations pursue their mission with such passion that they burn up their human resources, expecting them to sacrifice themselves for the sake of the mission. Our organizations and churches are filled with victims, people who are trapped between the articulated values of their community and the cultural realities of how they are treated. Sometimes this is because the organization is operating in a manner different from its stated values. Sometimes it is because the members of the church or organization have a different understanding of the stated values than the organization does. In both cases, there is conflict to be resolved.

Several years ago we released a person at Regent because he was not able to do the job for which he was hired. We released him after extended probation, special training and coaching. He was not able to complete the assignment we needed done. When we finally gave him notice, he and many of his friends around the college felt that we were violating biblical values. They claimed that the responsibility of Christian community meant keeping him when he could not fulfil his assignment. We spent considerable time underlining that community is an important and critical value and may require the 'second mile', but it does not supplant the mission that brings us together in the first place.

Community, for me, is a very highly regarded value; for Regent, it is a deeply entrenched cultural assumption. Culture in fact may constrain the implementation of the mission, but it is not the mission. Who are we? – The mission is still the driving force, the organizing principle that unifies people and resources. What is important to us? – The culture and values shape the way that people live together and utilize their resources in pursuit of the mission.

Schein argues that it is the responsibility of the leader to identify, reinforce or change the culture.[13] For me this responsibility goes beyond simple organizational strategy. I believe that we are called to model in our organizational and community life the very fruit of the Spirit that we teach and preach from our faith. Our touch must match our voice.

This is something I have been working on at Regent College for over eleven years. I would like to believe that we have made progress, but I confess immediately that we are far from being an organization that lives what it believes. We try. We fail. We forgive and keep trying. As long as I am at Regent, I pray that we will always keep trying to be who we say we are.

When I first arrived at Regent, I called a meeting of the total college staff. I articulated my vision of the college as a community, invited comment, and sought to encourage dialogue and constructive criticism – caring confrontation. Committed to a relational model of leadership, I encouraged staff members to talk back to me and the other managers. This was the way I had always worked. They could not do it. No one would speak up. No one would criticize anything. No one offered any constructive ideas for anything. When I pushed further, I was told that staff members had learned over the years that it was not appropriate to talk back to administration. According to one staff person, 'It is not appreciated and is considered a violation of community. It might even cost you your job.' Earlier administrations would deny this was ever their policy or value. In fact they were hurt to hear this opinion. But whether they intended it to be true or not, the cultural beliefs that controlled the employees said very loudly, 'Keep quiet, don't rock the boat!' Regardless of how much I stated that things had changed, that speaking out was a sign of ownership and community accountability and was valued highly, the staff would not give feedback or constructive criticism. The culture had such a strong grip that they would not believe my stated values as the new president.

We had a breakthrough several months later when we hired a new person, who did not yet know the culture. She believed my stated values and started arguing and speaking out when invited to her first staff meeting. She pointed out all kinds of problems facing the staff that were not being addressed. The older members of staff were shocked and apologized to me for her impertinence! But she gave me the opportunity to praise her publicly for her commitment and ownership and, in that act, to reinforce the new culture. We acted on the problems she raised and in this way reinforced the stated values as accurately reflecting the new culture.

Over the first year, we moved most of the staff to a point where they would confront me with issues and proposed solutions. They were willing to accept ownership and look for solutions rather than only see problems. Interestingly, the culture changed first around me. For the first year, staff would only talk back to me. They did not really believe that their managers who had been part of the old culture would live with the new values. During the next year, we were able to move more of the feedback and participation into the leadership relationships between the staff and their managers. Now everyone talks back! And that is good. We increasingly have a community of owners who take responsibility for the mission and the community.

Another example of culture in many of our organizations forms around power and the making of decisions. Traditionally at Regent, academic decisions were made by consensus, reflecting the religious tradition in which the college was founded. Consensus was affirmed as a sign of community. Governance, however, remained officially (according to the by-laws) in the hands of the administration and the board. I was used to a model in which academic staff also participated in the governance of the college. I was very enthusiastic about introducing this model, but I was not willing to live with a consensus model for decision making. Too often consensus-style decision making leaves the power in the hands of the negative voice, not in hands of the community. I wanted a majority vote model that put the power in the hands of the academic staff as a group if they were going to participate as a group in governance.

We were talking about participation and community accountability. This was a culture issue. In Schein's terms it dealt with the nature of reality and truth and how decisions are made. Before I could involve the academic staff in governance, a basic cultural assumption had to be changed. We had to move to a belief in the appropriateness of arriving at 'truth', at a decision, by vote, legitimizing a person's right to vote 'no' and still support the group's decision. In many ways, it was a redistribution of power. We were taking the power away from a few strong individuals and giving it to the broader community.

It was interesting to watch the slow shift to a new cultural assumption. The decision to move to the new model was made by majority vote, but as no one voted against the change, it was in fact decided by consensus! The first real test came when two members voted against a motion that was supported by the majority of the academic staff. Several people wanted to reopen the discussion until the two hold-outs could be won over. The old culture still had a grip. The group were still resistant to deciding by majority. I intervened and encouraged the academic staff to give their colleagues the space to express their convictions and still support the decision. Both the individuals affirmed their support for the decision and there was a corporate sigh of relief. Since then I think everything we decide is decided by split vote! And it is not unusual for an issue that I believe in to be defeated in the corporate governing process. Power has been distributed. And yet even now, you can still feel the grip of the old culture. It is hard to move forward when conflicting views have been championed at a meeting.

One more story from my early Regent days, because it not only underlines what I am talking about but suggests that we are making progress.

At Regent College we have a receptionist, a switchboard operator. She tends to be the entry-level person on our staff. Traditionally, this was the position for which no one wanted to take responsibility. And yet this person is the voice and the first face of Regent. She or he is the first line in establishing the values. How the receptionist treats you when you call or walk in begins to form your relationship with Regent. That person can greatly affect your attitude and interests before you ever get to the president's office. It is a key role.

When I started at Regent, I moved the receptionist position into the president's office, not physically, but in terms of accountability. The receptionist was considered a member of my staff. I spent time with her, keeping her included and informed about events, activities and the plans of the college. I tried to articulate and model the kind of culture that was important to us and what I wanted her to communicate to people when they called or came in.

Even though I no longer supervise the receptionists, I do occasionally participate in the interview process, and I try to communicate regularly with them about the importance of their position. This position, perhaps more than any other, demonstrates the culture and values of the college. They need to understand this. And they do. We have had a string of very good switchboard-receptionists over the years and I regularly use them as illustrations of what I mean by modelling our values.

One year, however, I was talking about culture to a group of people and the receptionist was in the room. As usual, I referred to the importance of her position and the critical role she plays in establishing the culture of Regent. It was a good talk. However, afterwards she came up to my office and asked to see me. She said, 'I wish you wouldn't keep talking about the importance of my position when you speak!' I responded in surprise, 'Why not? It is important! You are the voice and face of Regent for many people.' Her response: 'That's not the issue. You tell everyone else how important I am to Regent, but you do not come down very often and tell me!' Well, she was right. I will not stop using the receptionist as an illustration, but I have clearly been confronted by someone who cared, and who showed me that I was not living up to my stated values. That behaviour must change. I need to tell the receptionist how important she is to the community as often as I tell others.

But note, while it was not very comfortable for me to hear that I was not fully living my values, it was encouraging to realize that the culture is taking hold. The very fact that she came to the president's office to share her concerns and feelings with me suggests a level of trust and ownership that I am pleased to see at Regent. Now, if I can just learn to do my part more consistently!

Articulating Personal Values

Each of us brings a set of personal values to our role in the organization and each of us in a leadership role reinforces an institutional culture, the values or the character of the organization, with each action, decision or policy. It is a worthwhile exercise to try to write out some of the values that you think you bring to your community. What is important to you? To what are you prepared to be held accountable in your leadership role? How do those values shape the way you want to live out your leadership?

I had a good illustration of personal values at work the last time my car was towed away. It was another cold and stormy morning in Vancouver, but I had an important meeting so I bundled up early and walked out to my car. It was gone! The construction crew working across the street had had it towed away – ticketed by the police and towed away, even more irritating.

The night before I had returned late from another important out-of-town meeting. I thought I had parked outside the temporary tow-away zone. I had not; in fact, I parked right under the sign! As you can imagine, this did not start my day well. To put it mildly, I was rather irritated. This was a major inconvenience. I needed to be at an important meeting on the future of theological education. But my car was towed.

When I learned the name of the towing company, I called to find where my car was. My Christian character was not obvious in my conversation! Yet when I hung up, I had to smile. The woman on the phone had handled me very well. I realized that the towing was my fault and that I could not blame her. She had managed to keep the conversation positive, light and even humorous.

When I got to the parking lot – a large dirty storage area with a wooden shack for an office – I had to wait in line for the woman to take care of other disgruntled executives whose cars were now in her possession. She managed them well also. When I reached the window, I told her that I thought she had handled me well. She replied: 'Thank you. Everyone who calls me or comes to this window is angry. My job is to see that it doesn't ruin their day!' Rather profound words on organizational culture and personal character from an entry-level clerk in a towing company shack! She was reflecting personal character with more integrity than the president of a theological school who stood at her window. And she was articulating a marvellous understanding of organizational culture or character as she focused on the people-building results of her work rather than the mechanics of her job. She saw value in her work and lived it well.

Everything the leader does reinforces the culture. As president of Regent, I am watched to see if I reinforce the organization's stated values. Do I live up to what I teach? How I behave is seen much more as institutional policy than what I say, and it reinforces the culture. Am I friendly or distant? Am I a workaholic or reasonably paced? Do I have presidential perks? A reserved parking space? Do I talk or listen? Do I keep my promises?

For five years I was a visiting lecturer at the University of Calgary's Executive Management Program. I was brought in to talk about vision and values in today's organizations. One year, one of the participants asked me what values I brought to Regent, to my leadership. I thought about this, and that

evening drafted a list of seventeen values as my first attempt
to write out my personal values for my leadership.

The seventeen values I listed that night related to people,
work and relationships. Here is my list:[14]

People

1. People have intrinsic worth
We need to value who they are as well as what they do. We
have to communicate dignity and worth. This is where we
stop to say 'thank you', to acknowledge our dependence
upon others.

2. Everyone should make a commitment to the mission
Again, I see the mission as the unifying force in an organization. It is around the mission that we come together, and all
members of the organizational community should make a
commitment and contribution to that mission.

3. People who work with us should grow
We should be making an investment in the people who invest
in our mission. In a small organization like Regent we have
very few layers. There is very little opportunity for promotion and growth in scope of responsibility. In our kind of
organization, I believe that turnover is a good thing. I would
rather invest in good people who move on than in poor
workers who stay. But I want everyone who does move on to
move on better equipped at what they do, better prepared to
serve wherever God takes them.

4. No one should take themselves too seriously
I regularly turn to Romans 12 for a reminder that we are all
in this together. Paul lists leadership as one of the gifts given
to the church, but it is not first. It falls between giving money
and showing mercy. Thus, if I can paraphrase Romans 12:3:
'Don't take yourselves too seriously.'

**5. All people should be treated as contributing peers regardless of
their scope of responsibility**
While we may pay at different levels because of competence,
experience or responsibility, every member of the organiza-

tion has something to offer and deserves to be valued for their contribution and their humanness.

6. Leadership should be empowering

This is what this book is about. Leadership is the process of giving power away, not collecting it. It is moving the power to influence into the hands of the people we are leading so that they can pursue the mission.

Work

7. The mission of the organization normally takes precedence over individual purposes

By this I do not intend to demean individual purposes or objectives. But I do want to remind us again that it is the mission that brings us together, and in the context of the organization personal agendas are always subordinated to the community agenda or mission.

8. Participation produces ownership of results

I commented on this in Chapter 2 when I looked at team building. It will show up again in the next chapter when we look at motivating people. I have found from experience what research is underlining daily: when people are involved they take ownership for the results. Participation is the best form of motivation.

9. The workplace should provide community

In today's world, the workplace and the church are the primary arenas for social relationships. As a leader, I believe I should encourage this – encourage the development of relationships that enable people to care for and learn from one another. As I noted above, community implies diversity and requires us to be inclusive in our thinking and our employment.

10. People should have fun and find joy in their work

Not all work is fun, but the community in which we work should be a place we enjoy. While a specific task may not be pleasant, people should be able to find joy in the mission to which they are contributing. I want people to look forward to Monday, not Friday! I want them to look forward to seeing their friends and belonging and contributing.

11. We should always provide professional service in a friendly environment

This was actually the motto of an institute I directed in California: friendly, professional service. We are in existence to serve. The needs of our constituents should be our first priority and we should serve them well. We should give them our best and do it with quality. And in line with the earlier value, we should be such a friendly place that people want to come back, even if just to say 'hello'.

Relationships

12. Truth is found in relationship

I do not have all the truth and I doubt if you do either. Together we can listen and learn. Personally, I put a very high value on relationship. It is in relationship that God reveals himself. It is in relationship that I learn how to interpret the truth around me. I do not assume that I have the truth. I seek to learn it in dialogue in relationship.

13. Information is friendly

No surprises. Openness. Everyone should know where I am going. Not everyone will agree with what I am doing at Regent, but no one can say they do not know what I believe and where I am trying to lead the institution. I share everything. I believe that the more people know, the more they become partners.

14. Confrontation is a sign of caring

As I noted above, community includes diversity and diversity means conflict. Confrontation addresses conflict by caring enough for the other person to engage them in a relationship in which both parties are held accountable to their stated values. If I really care about you, I will give you feedback on what I see and how I respond to it.

15. *Criticism without constructive action is destructive gossip*
We noted this in the Colossian case. Criticism usually holds you accountable to my values, rather than your own. And gossip occurs, I would argue, any time criticism is taken outside of the relationship. My definition of gossip is harsh. Anytime anything negative is said about someone to a third party without the permission of the person being talked about, it is gossip. And I think it is inexcusable, even when it happens in the context of prayer. I have great difficulty with people who need to give me a prayer request for someone else. That to me is a form of gossip. If I genuinely care about someone, I take the negative comment to that person directly. That is the only way the relationship can be healed and grow.

16. *Honesty, integrity and trust are essential in everything we do*
This is what followers look for in leaders. It is also what God expects from his people. We can hold ourselves to no lower standard than honesty and integrity. Only then will people give us their trust.

17. *Forgiveness should characterize our life together*
I listed this one last, but it is not the least important. There can be no leadership without forgiveness. Leadership involves the risk of making decisions when we do not really know what is best. This risk of leadership requires the context of forgiveness. Further, forgiveness is a prerequisite to empowerment. I am convinced that there is a direct correlation between forgiveness and empowerment. No one can be empowered without the freedom to fail. Forgiveness is freeing. It implies trust. It encourages risk, growth, leadership. I am not talking about freedom from consequences, but freedom to learn from failure and encouragement to try again. A culture of forgiveness encourages the risk of leadership. But even further, leaders need to be able to forgive themselves. We have a tendency to carry our mistakes around with us, as well as our uncertain decisions. We replay them in our minds, thinking of what we should have done. This paralyses our ability to take the risk of deciding and limits

our leadership. We must be prepared to live with consequences, but we have to be able to live with mistakes, to
forgive ourselves, if we are going to lead.

Whenever I list these values, I feel the need to make dis-
claimers. I do not consistently live up to this list, nor does
Regent College, but I am prepared to be held accountable to
these values. I expect to fail. I expect to be confronted by
someone who cares. I expect to be forgiven and encouraged
to try again.

As leaders we do bring values to the community, perhaps
articulated as I attempted to do, but definitely lived out in
everything that we do. Whether you take the time to write
them out or not, you are in fact living out of your own list
of deeply ingrained values. Our credibility as leaders is
directly tied to the congruence between our stated values
and the values reflected in our living – our voice and our
touch. To lead an organization to live as a Spirit-shaped
community, we must be willing to be held accountable to
live and lead as Spirit-shaped men and women of character.

Now, what might this look like when applied to an organization?

Articulating Corporate Culture: A Values Statement

The list of seventeen personal values I drafted for the Calgary
executives was published in the June 1991 issue of the *Regent
World*. They drew more comment than anything else I have
written, with letters from organizations both secular and
Christian at scattered locations around the world telling me
that they had became the basis for a variety of values statements. The Regent College strategic planning committee also
saw the list and asked me to draft a values statement to par-
allel our mission statement in our institutional publications.
This was what I was waiting for. It was a chance for the
College to articulate a set of shared values that we could
together reinforce and embed in the culture for decades to
come.

So several years ago I tried my hand at drafting what I call the *Character of a College*. It was a much more difficult process than I would have imagined. I should have remembered Max DePree's words in *Leadership Jazz*: 'The organization expects the leader to define and express both in writing and especially through behavior the beliefs and values of the institution. This may not be easy, but like many disciplines, it's essential. Writing down what an institution values makes everyone come clean. It can also make people uncomfortable. The safety of vaguely known beliefs will disappear pretty fast.'[15]

I spent considerable time preparing a first draft. It is one thing to list seventeen values. It is quite another to flesh them out in a form that can stand the test of community scrutiny and accountability. When I finished, I had produced something that I believe in deeply. In many ways it is an expression of my soul. However, when it was circulated, the common response was, 'Maybe in heaven!' What I found to be a compelling document, pulling me to live out a set of values, was seen by nearly everyone else as too complicated, too idealistic, or too threatening. No one wanted to vote against anything in the statement, but no one was prepared to put it in print as something to which we should be corporately held accountable. I tried to revise it but found myself personally committed to each point. I am prepared to be held accountable to each of these items, even though I expect to fail regularly.

After a year of discussion, it was decided that we did need such a statement at Regent, but that it should be much simpler. In the end we settled for four core values: personal spiritual growth and maturity; biblical scholarship; experienced Christian community; and vocational integration. These became the official stated values that we want to shape our mission and our corporate life together. That was as precise as our community was prepared to be during that round of planning.

However, the *Character of a College* still exists. It still represents the kind of community I want to be part of. I still distribute it, not as a Regent statement, but as a statement of my personal commitments, a statement of what I am trying to model at Regent and an articulation of that to which I am still willing to be held accountable. Interestingly, people are starting to ask for copies, and I do regularly see behaviours modelling the commitments of the statement. Recently the chairman of the board suggested that I have a copy framed and hung in the president's office as a reminder to others of my vision for Regent. Maybe we will emerge with a more detailed statement of values during our next planning process. Until then, this 'unofficial' *Character of a College* is what I have in mind when I talk about a values statement for our organizations.

This is my attempt to articulate a statement of values for Regent College. It shows the influence of Paul's letter to the Colossians on my thinking. I encourage you to try to draft such a statement for your organization. It is the first step in the process of surfacing the cultural assumptions and beliefs that shape our actions as we attempt to put in writing those values to which we are committed

Many 'cultural' questions are raised when we try to understand the culture of our organization. As we work through these and identify the shared value commitments, we pave the way for a statement of values that captures our intentions and focuses our leadership. How is conflict resolved in your community? How are people valued and affirmed? How are people disciplined, released? What does kindness mean when you must release someone? What does love mean when someone has a different view? How is the receptionist perceived? How is the leader perceived? What is the culture of leadership – reactive or proactive, entrepreneurial or bureaucratic? Is community defined by inclusiveness or exclusiveness? Is the culture written or oral? How is information disseminated? Does conflict produce confrontation or criticism? What is expected from God?

Creating and reinforcing the culture is a key responsibility of leadership. It is a long-term process. It requires a long-range commitment by the leadership. Without an organizational crisis, I am not convinced that a leader can permanently embed values in less than ten years! It requires

The Character of a College

Regent College seeks to be a learning and nurturing community of faculty, staff, students, board and senate, where the presence of God in Jesus Christ through his Holy Spirit is manifest in the human relationships, institutional policies and organizational procedures of the community.

I. **A Community of Thanksgiving**
 A. a place of prayer and thanksgiving, acknowledging our dependence upon God;
 B. a place of joy, where we relax in the security of God's love;
 C. a place where every organizational or community operation is an act of worship before God;
 D. a place where we meet God, gaining a biblical perspective on our personal identity and calling;
 E. a place where we acknowledge in gratitude those gifts entrusted to our stewardship.

II. **A Community of Wisdom**
 A. a place where we seek wisdom to see this world from God's perspective;
 B. a place where we seek truth with intellectual rigour and critical minds;
 C. a place where we have space to think and grow;
 D. a place where we are listened to;
 E. a place where knowledge is informed by biblical spirituality;
 F. a place where we bring together the varied pieces of our lives under the lordship of Christ.

III. **A Community of Character**
 A. a place of love, where we learn the importance of interdependent community;
 B. a place characterized by integrity, encouraging honesty and trust;
 C. a place of peace, where we can explore ideas with strife-free critique;
 D. a gentle place, where people and procedures nurture and encourage, where facilities and policies have compassion;
 E. a kind place, where we care actively for one another in true humility;
 F. a place of patience, where we are accepted as we are and encouraged to become what God intends us to be;
 G. a place where we see Jesus when we see one another.

IV. **A Community of Service**
 A. a place where we are empowered to develop our gifts in the service of others;
 B. a place where we are encouraged to live for Christ, bringing love and justice into the world;
 C. a place where we are equipped to make a difference in the market place and public forum;
 D. a place that serves in partnership with the local church;
 E. a place where cooperation is initiated;
 F. a place where mercy takes service the second mile.

V. **A Community of Forgiveness**
 A. a place of forgiveness and second chances;
 B. a place of trust, of God, of others, and of ourselves;
 C. a place where lives and relationships are healed;
 D. a place where failure is never final;
 E. a place of renewal and growth;
 F. a place of mercy and hope.

VI. **A Community of Commitment**
 A. a place where commitments are made and promises kept;
 B. a place driven by vision rather than efficiency;
 C. a place where the present is shaped by the future as well as the past;
 D. a place of accountability where responsibility takes precedence over rights;
 E. a place where stewardship replaces ownership;
 F. a place where excellence requires continual renewal;
 G. a place where the unity of community is continually reformed by the diversity of individual contributions;
 H. a place preparing to stand before God.

patiently walking with people, modelling and reinforcing the new culture. It requires leaders of vision who can see what God wants to accomplish with their organization and what their church or organization can look like with Christ present in its midst. It requires relational leaders who make themselves vulnerable by making an accountable commitment to a stated set of values. It requires servant leaders who have learned to depend upon God and expect to see God at work in their organizations in the years ahead. Vision, values and vulnerability – *maybe that is what relational servant leadership is all about.*

Conclusion: The Prayer of Forgiveness

We cannot talk about organizational culture and the leader's responsibility to articulate the corporate values of the community, model those values and reinforce them in the fabric of the culture without coming back to the leader. The character of the leader is reflected when leadership seeks to influence the culture of the organization. If that were the end of it, we might all choose not to lead. As hard as we try, our character is flawed. We fail to live up to the calling that God places before us. We fail and must be forgiven. Is that good enough? Can I hope to transform the culture of my organization with my biblical commitments when I struggle to live them out consistently in my own life?

It is at this point that I take great comfort in David's anguished cry before God: '*Have mercy on me, O God, according to your unfailing love*' (Ps. 51:1). Without forgiveness there is no hope for leadership. And I do not mean just the forgiveness of the people, of the organization, when our risk taking is wrong. That forgiveness is critical and is required for leadership to be effective, but what I am talking about here is more fundamental. It is the forgiveness of God that we need if we are to be audacious enough to stand up and lead the people of God when we know that we do not live up even to the marks of character that we read about in Colossians.

David was a leader chosen and used by God. His escapades are described well in the Old Testament. And his failures are recorded for all time. The story of his failure with Bathsheba is well known. With a devastating lack of character, David pursues Bathsheba into adultery and murder. The King has fallen. God's leader has failed. And yet even as I look at this moral collapse, I am fascinated and encouraged by the last words of David on his deathbed. These words are recorded in 2 Samuel 23:1-5:

These are the last words of David:
'The oracle of David son of Jesse, the oracle of the man exalted by the Most High, the man anointed by the God of Jacob, Israel's singer of songs:
'The Spirit of the Lord spoke through me; his word was on my tongue. The God of Israel spoke, the Rock of Israel said to me: "When one rules over people in righteousness, when he rules in the fear of God, he is like the light of morning at sunrise on a cloudless morning, like the brightness after rain that brings the grass from the earth."
'Is not my house right with God? Has he not made me an everlasting covenant, arranged and secured in every part? Will he not bring to fruition my salvation and grant me my every desire?'

Powerful words from one who failed God so blatantly. At the end of his life, in spite of all his struggles, acknowledging his weakness and failures, David can say, 'I was chosen by God,' 'God spoke through me,' 'Because I was dependent upon God, people were empowered by my leadership,' and most poignantly, 'I am forgiven; I trust in the covenant love of my God.' Only in dependence upon God and in recognition of needed forgiveness, can we dare to accept the responsibility to lead those to whom God sends us.

This recognition of David's failure and acknowledgement of God's forgiveness gives me hope – a hope that takes me to my knees continually in prayer – prayer that regularly finds expression in Psalm 51. This prayer of David shortly after Nathan's caring confrontation provides a model for men and

women in leadership, who know they survive only as long as
God chooses to 'create in them a new heart and renew a
steadfast spirit within them'. It seems fitting to end this
chapter on personal and organizational character with the
powerful prayer of a very human leader:

> Have mercy on me, O God,
>   according to your unfailing love;
>   according to your great compassion
>   blot out my transgressions.
> Wash away all my iniquity
>   and cleanse me from my sin.
> For I know my transgressions,
>   and my sin is always before me.
> Against you, you only, have I sinned
>   and done what is evil in your sight,
>   so that you are proved right when you speak
>   and justified when you judge.
> Surely I was sinful at birth,
>   sinful from the time my mother conceived me.
> Surely you desire truth in the inner parts;
>   you teach me wisdom in the inmost place.
> Cleanse me with hyssop, and I shall be clean;
>   wash me, and I shall be whiter than snow.
> Let me hear joy and gladness;
>   let the bones you have crushed rejoice.
> Hide your face from my sins
>   and blot out all my iniquity.
> Create in me a pure heart, O God,
>   and renew a steadfast spirit within me.
> Do not cast me from your presence
>   or take your Holy Spirit from me.
> Restore to me the joy of your salvation
>   and grant me a willing spirit, to sustain me.
> Then I will teach transgressors your ways,
>   and sinners will turn back to you.
> Save me from bloodguilt, O God,
>   the God who saves me,
>   and my tongue will sing of your righteousness.

O Lord, open my lips,
and my mouth will declare your praise.
You do not delight in sacrifice, or I would bring it;
you do not take pleasure in burnt offerings.
The sacrifices of God are a broken spirit;
a broken and contrite heart,
O God, you will not despise.
In your good pleasure make Zion prosper;
build up the walls of Jerusalem.
Then there will be righteous sacrifices,
whole burnt offerings to delight you;
then bulls will be offered on your altar.

Notes

[1] Oscar Hijuelos, *Mr. Ives' Christmas* (New York: HarperCollins, 1995).

[2] James M. Kouzes and Barry Z. Posner, *Credibility* (San Francisco: Jossey-Bass, 1993), 59.

[3] Warren Bennis, *On Becoming a Leader* (Reading, Mass.: Addison-Wesley, 1989), 40, 51.

[4] Kouzes and Posner, *Credibility*, 51ff.

[5] Max DePree, *Leadership Jazz* (New York: Doubleday, 1992), 1–3.

[6] Terrence E. Deal and Allen A. Kennedy, *Corporate Cultures* (Reading, Mass: Addison-Wesley, 1982); Thomas J. Peters and Robert H. Waterman, Jr., *In Search of Excellence* (New York: Harper & Row, 1982); Craig R. Hickman and Michael A. Silva, *Creating Excellence* (New York: New American Library, 1984); Tom Peters and Nancy Austin, *A Passion for Excellence* (New York: Warner Books, 1989); Tom Peters, *Thriving on Chaos* (New York: Knopf, 1987); DePree, *Leadership Jazz*; Kouzes and Posner, *Credibility*; J. Michael Fuller, *Above the Bottom Line* (Toronto: Macmillan Canada, 1993); James O'Toole, *Leading Change* (San Francisco: Jossey-Bass, 1995).

[7] Edgar H. Schein, *Organizational Culture and Leadership* (San Francisco: Jossey-Bass, 1992^2), 2.

[8] Schein, *Culture*, 12.

[9] Schein, *Culture*, 95.

[10] Schein, *Culture*, 95–96.

[11] Schein, *Culture*, 96.

[12] Schein, *Culture*, xiv, 2.
[13] Schein, *Culture*, 5.
[14] This list was published in Fuller, *Bottom Line*, 164.
[15] DePree, *Leadership Jazz*, 26.

Chapter V

Influencing through Relationships

Power, Purpose and Relationship

To launch our discussion about motivating and empowering people, we should remember Jude's fourth image: 'Wild waves of the sea, foaming up their shame.' In this potent picture, Jude captures power and purpose and relationship. These self-appointed leaders were making a big splash, but they were not going anywhere. They were grabbing attention with the roar of pounding waves, but they left nothing of value behind. As the tides of their leadership receded there was nothing but debris and destruction on the shorelines of their community. These were persons who used their power and position to point to themselves, to further their own interests, but they lacked purpose. Their energy was not useful. It tore down and eroded like an unruly sea. They were basically concerned with themselves, with their leadership, not with the people whom that leadership should be serving. They had not invested themselves in relationships with the people that might have allowed their energy to be channelled through others for the good of the community. All they offered was relentless churning without purpose or direction. Leadership is powerful, but it is power attached to purpose. Leadership exists to serve the mission and to serve the people. It is a relationship of power to serve.

Biblical leadership is a relationship – a long-term relationship modelled on God's patient working out of his

> Leadership is a relationship of dependency upon people.

purpose in our lives. Leadership is a relationship that cares enough to walk patiently with people towards a shared purpose. Leadership is not about leaders; it is about the people we lead.

Tychicus: Caring about Relationships

It is the people who make the Colossian story so compelling. We have been watching real people trying to work out their faith in their daily lives together. Now we will return to Colosse and look at the story through an unfamiliar set of eyes.

We see Paul writing with articulate theological persuasion, Onesimus beaming with new-found faith, and Philemon bristling with hostility. Into that mess walks Tychicus. Paul writes the letters and gives both letters and Onesimus to Tychicus and tells him, 'Now you go to Colosse and sort this out.' Does that feel like a familiar situation?

Positionally, Tychicus is not the leader. At best he is a member of the team, a member of Paul's immediate circle of friends, a volunteer into whose hands Paul's vision is entrusted. It's all theory and plans until it gets into Tychicus' hands. He has to make it work. Tychicus represents for me the essence of followership. He is the employee, the staff member, the volunteer. He is the one empowered by Paul to carry the mission to its appropriate conclusion. If leadership is about empowering people to own and implement the mission, Tychicus is the classic example of the empowered follower – the purpose of the leadership relationship.

We don't know very much about Tychicus. In Colossians 4:7–8 Paul says:

> Tychicus will tell you all the news about me. He is a dear brother, a faithful minister and fellow servant in the Lord. I am sending him to you for the express purpose that you may know about our circumstances and that he may encourage your hearts.

In this brief description, Paul tells us five things about Tychicus. He is a dear brother, faithful minister, fellow servant, trusted communicator and an encourager of people. Not bad titles to have behind any of our names!

- *Tychicus is a dear brother*
  He shared in the *koinonia*, the community of believers that made up the body of Christ. As we have seen, this is an important theme for Paul in both of these letters as he appeals to Philemon and the Colossians to live out their participation in *koinonia*, their membership in the community. It is this bond that links Paul, Philemon, Onesimus, Tychicus and the Colossians together. There are different roles to be played in the drama, but a common participation in the community of Christ.

- *Tychicus is a faithful minister*
  He did his job well, and because of that Paul entrusts him with the life of Onesimus and, in a critical way, with the spiritual growth of the Colossians. How Tychicus presents the letter and Onesimus, how he carries out Paul's instructions, will have a major role in shaping the response of Philemon and the Colossians. So, too, with every person we seek to lead. How they respond to our influence and carry out their responsibilities determines the effectiveness of our leadership. This is also true for leaders. How leaders serve the people entrusted to them will have a significant impact on the people's growth and the accomplishment of the mission.

- *Tychicus is a fellow servant in the Lord*
  The mission of the kingdom controlled all that he did. His life was given in service to God, to glorify God in Christ. All of his work was a reflection of that commitment. As one called to be a servant of the Lord, Tychicus was in fact a servant of the mission and a servant of the people. He accepted the purpose for which Paul wrote the letters and he gave himself to this task. In service to Paul, he accepted this assignment and in so doing offered himself in service to Onesimus, Philemon and the Colossian church. Nowhere is the leadership relationship more clearly

modelled than in the unassuming, almost hidden service of Tychicus.

I remember interviewing two people for a faculty position. When we were through, the choice seemed clear. One person had introduced us to himself and his programme, the other had introduced us to God, passing quickly over his own significant gifts and accomplishments. Who do people see when they walk into our offices? Who are we seen to be serving?

- *Tychicus is a trusted communicator*
  Paul is in prison. He has no telephone or FAX machine. No e-mail. No way to communicate the details of his situation, the frustrations and the hopes, the challenges and the fears. But he has Tychicus. He has a close trusting relationship with Tychicus. Paul trusts him with the letters, he trusts him with Onesimus and he trusts him to represent Paul accurately. Paul has invested in a relationship with Tychicus that enables him to serve Philemon, Onesimus and the Colossians through Tychicus. This is what the leadership relationship is all about. This connected web of relationships between Paul, Philemon, Onesimus and the Colossian church, with Tychicus in the centre, is the prototype for relational servant leadership. Who is the leader? Who is the follower? Who is the servant? Who is being served? Relational leadership is about leaders who are followers, followers who are leaders, servants who lead, and leaders who serve. Leadership is a relationship of mutual interdependency.

- *Tychicus is an encourager of people*
  What other kind of person could Paul send into this situation? Tychicus cares for people and works to build them up, to encourage them in their faith, in their work, in their personal lives.

  Throughout this drama we have seen the importance of relationships for Paul. Paul appeals to his relationship with Philemon to persuade and encourage Philemon. Paul emphasizes his relationship with Onesimus to give

Onesimus credibility. Paul expects Philemon and Onesimus to be reconciled because of their common faith, and he expects that reconciliation to be encouraged by the broader Colossian community. But think also of the relationship between Tychicus and Onesimus. Think of the trust that Onesimus must have in Tychicus, who in many ways holds Onesimus' life in his hands. If Tychicus does not take this seriously, Onesimus is the one who loses. But think also of the benefits of that trust. Onesimus must go back, but he does not go back alone. He has a friend going with him. Tychicus is there to support and encourage Onesimus as much as to challenge Philemon and the church. Paul has a vision. Tychicus implements that vision. That is what the leadership relationship is all about.

Tychicus, a dear brother, a faithful minister, a fellow servant, a trusted communicator and an encourager of people – a critical player in the drama of Paul and the Colossian church. Paul knew what he wanted to accomplish, but he was dependent upon Tychicus to make it happen.

The Care and Nurture of Paid and Unpaid Staff

Leadership is a relationship of dependency. Leaders articulate vision. Leaders reinforce values in all they do. But leaders are dependent upon other people to make it happen. In this chapter I look at the leadership relationship in terms of the care and nurture of the people through whom we accomplish our vision and with whom we live out our values. This is the point where the relational character of servant leadership is most visible. In the interdependent relationship of leader and follower we hear the heartbeat of servant leadership most clearly.

I want to sketch the basic components of a human resource management system as developed by the corporate and non-profit or service sectors. However, to underline the importance of relationship in leadership, I would like to look at a people development model primarily from the perspective of a volunteer. I choose this approach for several reasons. First, I believe that all human resource management principles and processes apply to unpaid workers or volunteers. Second, with the development of portfolio lifestyles, we will increasingly find ourselves employing volunteers in our organizations as well as our churches. Third, as leaders and followers we will increasingly find our own self-expression and ministry in volunteer service. Finally, I agree with Max DePree[1] who argues that nearly all employees today are essentially volunteers. They choose to stay in their current jobs. They are not bound to a particular position. DePree argues that people stay with Herman Miller or our organizations because they believe we offer them a fair return on their invested time and effort. When they believe to the contrary, they begin to look elsewhere for employment. In that sense all workers are volunteers. Think about it. Do you stay in your present position primarily for the money? Probably not. Do you remain in this position because you have no other options? Again, not likely. We *choose* to do what we do. We *choose* to stay in the position in which God has currently placed us. To that extent we are volunteers. Daily we *choose* to be where we are.

Management books and journals talk about paradigm shifts and the new information age. This is one of the paradigm shifts: People no longer (if they ever did) stay in a position out of loyalty to a company or organization. Organizations no longer promise to take care of their people for the length of their careers. Things are changing so fast that no one can coast. Organizations cannot afford to keep people who simply do the job they used to do the way they used to do it. Organizations need people who are learning and growing and changing with the organization and its environment. At the same time, people can no longer learn a skill or gain a level of knowledge and ride it out for life. What we know and do today may well be obsolete tomorrow. We all must keep learning and growing in order to continue to make a contribution in the changing context of our organizations.

Fast Company: How Smart Business Works is a new journal for the young workers of the information age. Pick up any issue and see the headlines screaming this new reality: 'The Brand Called You', 'Free Agent Nation', 'You Decide', 'The Talent Market', 'The War for Talent', 'Hire Today ... Gone Tomorrow'.[2] The initiative is with the follower. The choice belongs to the follower. To be employable – whether as a paid employee or as a volunteer – we must keep learning and growing. Those who do are the people for whom every organization is looking.

But this new paradigm, this new reality, puts a burden on both people and organizations. Organizations have to take active leadership in the recruitment and retention of their employees – their volunteers – their free-agent-temporary-contract-service-providers. Recruitment is never finished. It is an ongoing responsibility. At the same time, people must keep themselves renewed and growing to contribute to changing organizational environments and goals. They must take responsibility for their own learning and growth. Those who cannot keep up will find themselves marginalized. The opportunities for contribution and growth are escalating, but so is the probability of unemployment and economic despair.

This presents a new challenge for leadership. Leadership, as I have said, serves both the mission and the people. These two 'services' will be increasingly in tension. The mission is served by embracing gifted people who own the mission and continually renew their own ability to contribute as the mission is renewed. Leaders must focus first on the mission that defines the organization. At the same time, leaders must recruit good people and so invest themselves in the growth and development of these people that the team members will both be able to contribute over the long run and will also find the organizational setting a place in which they want to invest themselves for the long run. Leadership is a relationship of service to the people that continually renews them and re-engages them in the life of the organization.

Another reason for looking at the topic of people development through the eyes of a volunteer is that this is the point at which most organizations totally fail to develop their people. The best organizations take their paid human resources very seriously, seeking to develop them as individuals and as resources. Unfortunately, too many organizations do not care for their people well. Religious organizations have a reputation, in fact, for not taking their paid employees seriously and practically abusing their volunteers. Focusing on the leadership relationship from the perspective of the volunteer enables us to identify important issues that are key to the motivation and leadership of all members of our organizations.

However, even with volunteer programmes, it is difficult to find good models. Over the years, I have encountered a few organizations that take volunteers very seriously. I have been particularly impressed with the way volunteers are developed at the Los Angeles zoo, American Red Cross, Sierra Club, Huntington Memorial Hospital in Pasadena, and the Los Angeles Olympics. Hospitals seem to have done a better job than most organizations in developing volunteer programmes that attract and retain good people who find there an outlet for their gifts and values. Churches, on the other hand, utilize more volunteer resources than any other kind of organization but are notorious for the lack of relational investment in their volunteers.

Everything we will explore in this chapter about managing human resources – about developing people – applies equally to volunteers, paid staff, profit and non-profit organizations, and the local church. I will use the term *volunteer* to represent all team members – paid and unpaid – to remind us that the follower *chooses* to follow.

Why people volunteer

Why do people volunteer? Why do they choose to spend their time and talent with a particular organization? There are many reasons. People volunteer to gain love and acceptance. They volunteer to gain recognition and status, to have power. They may join because an organization gives them an opportunity to influence decisions that affect them. People volunteer to be important. Once when I was leading a workshop in Washington, D.C., I did the usual tourist things and visited the various monuments. In the tall Washington

Monument, I met Jerry. Jerry is an elevator operator in the Washington Monument. He volunteers eight to ten hours per week. He is very pleased to be part of this historic centre in his country. He pointed to his 'volunteer' cap with pride and told me that he had to be active at least ten hours each month to keep his 'status'. How many of the people in your organization are worried about losing their volunteer status?

People volunteer to find self-fulfilment and growth. Sharon worked as a volunteer in children's ministries to give meaning to her life that she could not find in her paid work. Some volunteer for self-expression. Beverly volunteers as the gardener at a home for the physically challenged because she loves to garden and lives in a condominium. People also volunteer to explore paid employment. Florence volunteers for the church library because she wants to go into library science when her children have grown.

People volunteer to promote a cause they believe in, to make things happen, or because they want to be 'where the action is', part of something that is making a difference. Ron volunteers as a political worker to promote his views on government. Jean volunteers as an assistant in a continuing education programme because she wants to see educational resources made available to persons who cannot come to traditional schooling. Elizabeth volunteered as director of alumni services at Regent because this area had been significantly underdeveloped and she wanted to change that.

People volunteer to 'be with my kind of people'. They volunteer as much for the social connectedness as for the actual task. Who they get to work with is very important to many who join our organizations. People also volunteer to serve others, to feel good about the investment they are making in other persons.

And finally, behind all of these reasons, we hope that people are also investing in our organizations because they want to serve God. They see our organization – our community – as one place they can work out their calling before God. I put this reason last because it is the one that frequently sidetracks Christian leaders, especially pastors. I have heard many pastors articulate a belief that I should volunteer

to serve God and accept the assignment they have in mind as
an expression of my gratitude to God. I want to counter this
argument by noting that I am grateful to God and I do work
for pay and volunteer to serve God. I do believe that all that
I do is an outworking of my calling as a minister of Jesus
Christ. However, I do not believe that necessarily means I
should work in your church in that assignment. Show me
how the position for which you want me to volunteer will
serve me as I seek to invest my limited hours in a way that
fulfils my calling to serve God. There are many places a volunteer can invest gifts and time and still be serving God.
Leaders need to take the relationship seriously, serving the
volunteer as they serve the mission.

This is an important principle for the leading and motivating of people. There is an exchange that takes place in every
volunteer relationship. Volunteers, paid and unpaid, have
something to give. But there is also something that they
want, a need that must be addressed. This is important.
There is a reason why they are willing to give their time and
their talent. Relational leadership takes that seriously. In
Canada, where social policies have led to less emphasis on
volunteering than in the United States, organizations are just
beginning to realize that people give their time by choice. An
article in *The Vancouver Sun*[3] a few years ago noted that
people these days volunteer for a reason. They engage in the
volunteer relationship for the exchange, not just to volunteer. As the government pulls back on services and the volunteer sector begins to emerge, the exchange embedded in
the volunteer relationship is also surfacing as an important
focus for the leadership of volunteers. To the extent that we
understand the exchange with our volunteers, we will be able
to address their needs, motivate them and nurture their contribution to our organization.

The point I want to make here is that there is an
exchange. Volunteers – all workers – want something out of
it. They cannot be taken for granted. Volunteers want a
return on the investment of their time. This is a foundational principle for the management of people, paid or
unpaid. Only when we recognize this truth can we begin to

lead people in a way that grows them and accomplishes our shared vision and values.

The recruitment and orientation of volunteers

The leadership relationship begins with recruitment. Recruitment is first of all a planning and communications problem. It is only when we know the organization's needs that we can communicate those needs with specificity in a call for volunteers.

Remember that we are not in the business of employing volunteers. We are organized for a mission. Therefore, we only want volunteers who will assist the organization in carrying out its mission. Consequently recruitment starts with planning. What are we trying to accomplish? What kind of staffing will it take to accomplish this? Specifically, what kind of person, what set of gifts and experience does the organization need in order to accomplish this piece of our mission? The recruitment of volunteers is always mission driven. It is the mission that determines what needs to be done. It is what needs to be done that determines our staffing needs. Volunteers are always recruited to achieve the mission.

The best source for volunteers is referral by other satisfied volunteers. We need to develop a reputation for being a good place to volunteer, a place that cares about the contribution and the growth of its people.

With volunteers, paid or unpaid, the recruitment process should involve an honest presentation of the needs of the organization as represented by the particular position for which the person is volunteering as well as a careful review of the person's gifts, interests, experience and abilities. For paid and unpaid positions, I always ask: 'Why do you want to work here?' I want to understand the exchange need and be sure that it is one we can and want to meet. We must be willing to turn down volunteers who are not qualified and move them to other opportunities for which they are qualified or train them for this position. This is hard for us to do in Christian organizations. We are very reluctant to turn anyone down, especially in unpaid positions. We are also afraid that we will not find anyone else. Yet the experience of successful volunteer agencies is precisely the opposite. Tightening the screening for a position only increases the importance of the position. It does not make it harder to recruit!

Susan is a docent in the Los Angeles zoo. She leads groups of children on tours of the zoo, and introduces the various animals. In order to obtain this volunteer position, Susan had to undertake ten weeks of study and a major qualifying examination and must complete annual training and retesting. What do you need to do to qualify to lead children in your church, to volunteer in your organization? Volunteer trip leaders for the Sierra Club must complete two rigorous training courses and keep their mountaineering skills up to date. If we want to keep people in our organizations, we must invest in their training regardless of their form of compensation. There is a myth that lingers over unpaid employment. We are afraid that if we make the qualifications too high, no one will volunteer. Not so. If the opportunity for service meets the exchange requirements of the volunteer, high qualifications only underscore the importance of the task. There is a waiting list for docents at the Los Angeles zoo.

Recruitment is about finding the best person to contribute to the organization's mission. Understanding and presenting the position in light of the mission is critical. It is also important, however, for leaders to understand the exchange need of the volunteer. Even with high-salaried volunteers, the exchange need varies depending on where that person is in their own life, career or ministry. Salary is seldom the issue in recruitment. Hours may be a concern. Colleagues – those with whom a person will be working – are often major issues in recruiting key individuals. Future potential is highly valued. My 30-year-old son left his established position as an attorney to join a financial consulting firm that offered him a stake in their future. Housing is a concern for organizations like Regent College that are located in areas where residential housing is very expensive. Schooling for children, transportation, sabbatical leaves, continuing education opportunities – all are issues that may need to be addressed in the recruitment process. For many of us in Christian communities, this is new. Long-term employees talk about the sacrifices they made when they joined the organization. New recruits want to nail things down in advance and want to explore all of the exchange needs up front. I was surprised when my 28-year-old son agreed to change jobs but requested a paid vacation the first month. I was more surprised when they gave it to him! Now after two years he is considering another move, and his company has offered a car and gasoline credit card for his commute. This is no longer unusual. It is the way the entrepreneurial generation of the 21st century thinks. The recruitment of people has become more complex in this changing 'talent-scarce economy'.[4]

When the right person is found for a position and the interdependent commitments of the exchange have been negotiated, the agreement of service should be spelled out in writing. Both the leader and the volunteer should have the same understanding of what is to be accomplished and the terms of the appointment.

Once a volunteer has been added to the team, there is usually a process of orientation to help the new member learn the way things are done in this organization – an introduction to the culture. Every volunteer has the right to a clear understanding of the organization, its vision and values, its ministries and its policies. This can be handled by a volunteer manual, an orientation programme, or both. At this point, especially in the United States, I refer churches and other organizations that employ volunteers to their nearest hospital. Most major hospitals have developed very sophisticated volunteer programmes, including a good volunteer manual, and usually an effective volunteer orientation programme.

A good manual is a valuable tool for orienting volunteers. The manual might include a letter of greeting from the president, pastor or chairperson of the board. It should have a description of the organization or church and its community and denominational relationships. It might include a brief description of programmes and services, and perhaps even an organizational chart that shows who is responsible for whose success. It might include the names and titles of board members and other staff, a current operating budget, policies and procedures for volunteers, volunteer job descriptions, the criteria for recognition as a volunteer, emergency procedures and phone numbers, and sample forms that will be used regularly. At Regent College we developed an extensive manual for our board that has become a model requested by many theological schools across North America. We also, of course, have the traditional handbooks for academic and administrative staff – paid and unpaid.

Once the need for a position has been established in the planning stage, a volunteer has been recruited to fill that position, and the orientation programme has drawn the new staff member into the organization, then the leadership relationship moves to the fore. The focus now is on the motivation and nurture of the volunteer.

The CARE Plan

It is fitting now that we return to the heart of leadership – the relationship between the leader and the follower. It is in the context of this leadership relationship that we are able to influence people in a way that empowers them to contribute to the shared mission of our organizations and enables them to grow in their own competence and confidence.

I want to describe this leadership relationship using a simplified human resource development model that I call the CARE Plan for Volunteer Development. This model is built around four common-sense responsibilities of leadership: *C*larify expectations; *A*gree on objectives; *R*eview progress; and *E*quip for performance and growth.

Clarify expectations

Here we look at two things: job descriptions and performance standards.

1. Job descriptions
Everyone has a right to know what they are doing! I realize this is a rather simplistic common-sense statement, but it is

often ignored. This is what job descriptions or position descriptions are all about – letting a person know what their job is, what they are supposed to be doing. In the best of organizations, job descriptions are often treated as a necessary evil – the paperwork of bureaucracy. In volunteer organizations like the local church, job descriptions are practically non-existent. I would argue that job descriptions should be prepared for every position in a church or organization, full- or part-time, paid or unpaid.

A job description is a written record of the duties, responsibilities and requirements of the position. It answers the question: What is my job? It should describe the job carefully and identify the tasks the person is expected to perform. It should identify the limits of responsibility and authority. It should be specific and brief.

The amount of detail in a job description is directly related to the responsibility of the position. The more responsible the position, the more broadly responsibility and authority are assigned. The description does not spell out specific tasks, but defines the skills and abilities needed and leaves room for initiative in how tasks will be carried out. The less responsible the position, the more specifically the duties, time and skills are spelled out – exactly what needs to be done and when.

The job description for the Director of Church Relations at Regent College identifies the need for relational skills, the ability to drive oneself around the greater Vancouver area and the requirement to speak with a hundred pastors each year about the programmes of Regent College. It is a part-time position and the volunteer is given significant latitude in regard to time and approach. However, when we need an audio-visual assistant, we are not only precise about the skills needed, but we are very specific about the hours to be worked and what needs to be accomplished at specific times, for example, running the sound system during chapel every Tuesday from 11.00 to 11.45 a.m.

Do not get too complicated! Something simple that works is best. This is not about producing paper. It is about empowering the follower, the volunteer, to contribute to the mission. The job description is a tool designed to help both leader and follower understand what the organization requires of them. The objective is to produce a document that spells out, ideally in one page, what the leader and the follower understand as 'the job'. Over the years I have used a very simple form for getting started with job descriptions. We have used this form in a variety of churches and in a few organizations. It is a workable starting model. I do notice, however, that eventually, especially for more responsible positions, the description tends to become longer. Most of our senior positions at Regent now have two- to three-page descriptions. I am not convinced this is necessary, especially if we are preparing job descriptions in an organization where they have not been traditionally used.

The base model I start with, if the organization does not have another way of doing things, is a single page entitled *POSITION DESCRIPTION* with the following headings: Job title; Date established; Department; Supervisor; Relationship to mission; Duties, responsibilities and authority; Skills required; Time required; Training required and provided; Job location. It looks like this:

POSITION DESCRIPTION

Job title:

Date established:

Department:

Supervisor:

Relationship to mission:

Duties, responsibilities and authority:

Skills required:

Time required:

Training required and provided:

Job location:

---

(1) Job title.   This is simply the designation within the organization. What do we call this person? Director of Church Relations? A-V Assistant? President? It is a point of identification for the organization's records. I might note here that Tom Peters has commented on the power of titles in recognizing and motivating employees. Giving someone a title that accurately reflects a specific area of responsibility is more motivating than a generic title such as 'clerk'.[5]

(2) Date established.   This again is only for the organization's records. When was this position established?

(3) Department.   This provides context. It identifies how the person fits into the larger community of the organization, how the person will be part of the team. The Director of Church Relations is part of the Development Office of Regent. The A-V Assistant is part of the Administration Office. Similarly an assistant Sunday School teacher may belong to the Christian Education Department.

(4) Supervisor.   This one is important. Who is responsible for the success of this person? I will come back to this point below, but for now I would assert strongly that if you cannot identify the supervisor, no one should accept the job! The Vice-President for Development is responsible for the success of the Director of Church Relations. The Director of Audio-visual Services is responsible for the A-V Assistant. But, again, we will come back to this one.

(5) Relationship to mission.   What I look for here is a description of the responsibilities or contributions of this position in terms of the organization's mission. Why is this position important? How does it contribute to the larger mission of the organization? Completing this part of the job description is a reminder to both the leader and the follower that the position was established to serve the mission of the church or organization. The position exists as an important part of the larger mission and strategies. It is not there for the benefit of the leader or the follower but for the mission. That

may seem like an insignificant point, but it can become important in the leadership relationship if both the leader and the follower recognize that they are there to serve the mission. The follower is not there to serve the leader. In fact, as I will argue shortly, the leader is there to help the follower serve the mission. Defining the position and the leadership relationship in terms of the mission provides objectivity for the human dynamic within the relationship.

(6) Duties, responsibilities and authority. This is where the specific things that are to be accomplished by this position are spelled out. What precisely do we want the volunteer to do? What is this person responsible for accomplishing? What authority does this person have to carry out these responsibilities? What decisions should this person make on his or her own? When does this person need approval before proceeding? As I noted earlier, the detail here will be inversely proportional to the level of responsibility. The more responsibility, the less specificity. What we want is a list of responsibilities that will allow anyone picking up this job description to quickly understand this person's exact responsibilities.

(7) Skills required. What does this person need to be able to do to fulfil the requirements of the position? Type? Know a particular software programme? Is a driver's licence needed? Does the person need experience teaching? A certain level of education? These expectations need clarification before the leadership relationship begins.

(8) Time required. Here the follower deserves an honest assessment of the amount of time this assignment will require. This is especially important for unpaid volunteers who are giving the time and receive no overtime compensation. Clarifying this expectation is important both ways. The follower and the leader need to know the organization's expectations for the amount of time as well as the use of time. And the leader needs to understand the follower's expectations regarding how much time he or she is willing to invest in this position.

(9) Training required/provided. This item assumes that the organization is interested in the growth of its people and is investing in their continued training. It is a clarification of expectations that is important both ways. The volunteer or employee should know exactly what kind of training will be provided to enable him or her to complete the assignment and grow into more responsibility. At the same time the organization needs to make it clear if training will be provided in which the employee is expected to participate. I frequently hear churches complaining about the poor attendance of Sunday School teachers at their teacher training workshops. Usually I hear three reasons for this lack of attendance. First, they are scheduled at a time that volunteers are reluctant to give up – Saturdays. Second, the quality of the workshops often leaves something to be desired. Third, there was no clearly stated expectation that taking on the responsibility of teaching also meant accepting responsibility for attending a set number of training workshops. If volunteers are expected to participate in training, clarify this expectation in the job descriptions, schedule the training at a time designated by the participants, and make sure that the workshops are of such high quality that no one would want to miss them.

(10) Job location. This information is less critical but is included especially for unpaid volunteers. Where will the person work? Where do we expect him to carry out these responsibilities? Will she have an office? A classroom? Does the person work out of his house? Does she use her own car? These are the kinds of things that are best clarified up front in any leadership relationship.

This particular outline is obviously not definitive. It is one I have used effectively over the past years. If you have a better model that works, use it. If not, this is a basic outline to start with.

The job description is about the clarification of expectations. I am not promoting more paperwork, but I believe strongly that job descriptions are an important foundation for the leadership relationship. They make a difference. If the assignment we want someone to do is important enough to do, it is worth describing. If it is not worth the time to describe on one page, it is surely not worth anyone's time to do it.

If you find yourself in an organization or church without job descriptions, one way to start is to give everyone a blank job description form. Let them fill in the job description based on their experience of the job. Then have them sit down with their supervisor to clarify what the church or organization needs to see in that job description. If they understand their job well, job descriptions will be written in that process. If they do not understand their jobs well, you needed to have these discussions anyway! You need to clarify some expectations.

Once, when I was serving as the Chair of the Christian Education Committee of our church, we needed two teachers to supervise the toddlers during the main worship service. At that time we had not yet brought job descriptions into our church, but we announced the need for the teachers and began to look for some volunteers. No one volunteered. Finally a recommendation was brought to the committee that we should hire two persons (for money) to cover this critical assignment. Job descriptions were drawn up with expectations and compensation spelled out. Almost immediately we had three *volunteers* for the position. Once the church had said 'this responsibility is important enough to describe specifically and pay for', three people decided it was important enough for them to volunteer their time. That was the beginning of job descriptions for all of our volunteer positions at the church.

For years Doug had struggled to recruit volunteers for his church's Social Services Centre. Looking for help, he registered for a workshop I was leading on the care and motivation of volunteers. He said that he spent so much of his time recruiting new volunteers to staff the centre that he was not able to fulfil his responsibilities to the church. He still had two unfilled positions. If something did not change he would have to shut down the centre. The centre provided food, clothing and shelter for the homeless and others in need. He really did not want to shut it down. He completed the workshop and took the CARE Plan model back to the centre. He wrote to me nearly a year later to let me know how it worked. He said that he immediately drafted job descriptions for every position in the Social Services Centre, and posted the two openings. On the first Sunday after the postings were announced, he had eight new volunteers for the two positions. Now, one year later, he reported that volunteerism was up 35% over the past year; all positions were filled and he had a waiting list of volunteers. It works!

At the Huntington Memorial Hospital in Pasadena, California, there is a baby-rocking programme. This is a special programme for infants who must remain in the hospital without their parents. Volunteers are recruited to provide one hour per week rocking babies. They simply hold the little infants and rock them, letting them feel the physical presence of love. My wife saw an article about the programme in our newspaper and was immediately captured by the idea. The next day she went down to get a job description and to sign up as a volunteer. Every position was filled with a waiting list of 150 people! Now, think about that. How long is the waiting list in the nursery of your church? Same job; but look at the difference. The hospital says, 'This is an important ministry to babies and families; come, be part of this important ministry.' Too often the churches communicate: 'Will someone help keep these babies quiet while we get on with the real ministry over in the sanctuary?' See the difference. The hospital gives dignity and value to the work. Too many churches and organizations fail to give dignity and worth to the task they ask people to take on. Job descriptions are one simple and important way to underline the value of a job and give dignity to the assignment.

Gary attended a class on leadership and volunteers and designed job descriptions using the outline we just reviewed for every position in his church and had them approved by the church board. All of the job descriptions, from the part-time volunteer to the senior pastor, were bound together in a small photocopied booklet. The response amazed him. He saw people walk into the church, look at the booklet and comment to one another: 'Look, here I am; I'm in the same booklet with the pastor!' What seems like a small thing is in fact an important way to recognize the contribution of every player on our ministry teams and reinforce its value to our mission.

2. *Performance standards*

The job description clarifies the basic expectations for the position. However, if there are quality expectations or standards for the level of performance expected, these also should be clarified. What do you expect? What do you expect to see accomplished, over what time period, with what quality? How will you evaluate performance in this position? By what criteria will you know that the job is being done right? Performance standards focus on results and outcomes.

In our Christian circles there is too often a tendency to resist standards, measurement and accountability. However, as I have noted earlier, a reading of Ezekiel 34 or Jude 12–13 should call us up short. God seems to have clear expectations of those of us in leadership. Accountability and evaluation accompany responsibility. We need to understand what is expected of us as leaders and we owe the same clarification to the people we lead.

Several years ago a new manager told me that he wanted to fire one of his assistants. When I asked him if he had discussed it with her he said, 'No.' I told him he could not release her until they had gone over the organization's expectations for the position and had given her at least three months of closely reviewed time to help her succeed. He did this and reported back that no one had ever told her what was expected. She turned out to be his best employee once the expectations were understood. Clarify expectations. Give value and dignity to the work. Set up the standards by which volunteers can measure their progress as they seek to make a contribution to the mission of the organization.

Agree on objectives

All employees have a right to know what is expected of them. This means that each volunteer, every member of the team, must have a *supervisor* – someone assigned to support and enable the person to carry out his or her ministry. This is important! This is the core of relational leadership, of servant leadership. We are talking about leadership as an empowering service to those for whom the leader is responsible – not vice versa. Note how I keep repeating 'for whom the leader is responsible'. The leader is responsible for the success of the follower, paid or volunteer. In the leadership relationship, I prefer to ask 'for whose success are you responsible?' rather than the traditional 'who reports to you?' It keeps the flow of power moving in the right direction – from the organization through the leader to the follower for the accomplishment of the mission.

Leaders are responsible for the success of their followers. This is a fundamental principle of leadership for me. Early in the tenure of David Hubbard as president of Fuller Seminary, he found himself in conflict with members of his board. Max DePree, then a young member of the board, took Hubbard aside and told him, 'I am on your side in this matter and I will commit myself to your success as president of this school.' Many believe Hubbard's long and successful tenure at Fuller was because he had Max DePree in his corner for those thirty years. David Hubbard would have agreed. Would that everyone could have a leader, a supervisor, committed to their success.

That supervisor or leader can be a paid member of the team or an unpaid volunteer. Salary does not make one a leader. I should note in passing that *any position can be filled by an unpaid volunteer* as well as a paid volunteer. I know unpaid volunteers who are chief executive officers, chief financial officers, chief administrative officers, directors, consultants, teachers, directors of marketing, development, etc. There is no position that cannot be filled by a competent qualified volunteer, paid or unpaid, with a good job description and a leader responsible for his or her success.

'*No supervisor,*' says '*No one cares what I do.*' The volunteer and the supervisor together work out the specific objectives for the volunteer's assignment. What precisely do we want this person to do? These objectives should be spelled out on one page clearly enough that anyone would know exactly what the volunteer is expected to accomplish in the specified time frame. This becomes the standard by which the volunteer's progress and performance will be measured.

At Regent College, all employees, paid and unpaid, present a draft of their objectives for the year at the time of their performance review. In discussion with their supervisor, these objectives are revised as necessary based on the needs of the college. They then become the standard against which employees evaluate their own progress at the next review. Each year the senior management team prepares a draft of the key objectives for their departments to review with me and the management cabinet. I then compile these objectives into the President's Annual Plan, which is presented to the board with the annual budget. In the fall, each senior manager submits an evaluation of his or her department against the previous year's annual objectives. I compile this information into the President's Annual Report for review at the annual meeting of the Board of Governors.

In the leadership relationship, the leader or supervisor connects the follower, the volunteer, to the organizational mission. The leader is responsible for seeing that the volunteer succeeds in contributing to the mission. Through the establishment and review of objectives, the leader keeps the follower growing in that contribution.

Review progress

The third principle of this people development model focuses on evaluation. In human resource management this is called *performance review*. This is the area about which I have the strongest feelings. Unfortunately, it is the most misunderstood and abused component of people management. It is thought to be judgemental and critical, destructive to motivation. And it frequently is!

Performance review is intended to keep the organization's goals in focus. It is designed to assist the leader in developing employees or volunteers in their own growth towards leadership. It is intended to enable people to do their jobs to the best of their ability.

Performance reviews are tools for development and growth, not times for judging and criticizing, not times to give an annual grade. Leaders need training to do them well. Unfortunately, typical performance reviews do not involve caring confrontation, instead they are mere pats on the back accompanied by a reference to one area that is weak and needs improvement. In other words, 'You're OK, except in this area where you get a B.' Leaders give this kind of review because they have been told to conduct a review and because they feel that they need to be able to show followers where they still have room to grow. Leaders leave the review feeling uncomfortable. Followers leave this kind of review not feeling very encouraged and often angry. Volunteers or followers tend to forget all the positive things that are said and focus only on the negative areas noted as needing growth. Team members experience such reviews as criticism rather than affirmation. The way performance reviews are traditionally administered cause both leaders and followers to dread them and generally to leave unsatisfied.

Leaders should see performance reviews as checkpoints, not as times to criticize. Reviews provide opportunities to help followers develop skills, expand their contribution, advance their careers, and gain promotion in the organization because they are growing – in short, to become leaders in their own right. All of these outcomes can be accomplished while achieving the organizational goals.

Performance reviews are part of the personal and leadership development system – the feedback loop. They should provide information to the leader and the employee that will enable each to grow in their contribution to the organization. Performance reviews mean that someone cares. As I noted above, a job description says, *'This is an important part of our mission,'* and the assignment of a supervisor says, *'Someone cares what I do.'* The performance review suggests that *'Someone cares about me.'* It is part of the investment that the leader makes in the growth of the follower. It is a sign of caring.

This was brought home poignantly to me several years ago. In the office I was managing, I had been giving performance reviews to all of the team using my preferred model. At that time I only conducted performance reviews with full-time employees. Nancy had worked with me for three years as a senior seminar coordinator. We had been through three reviews together. In her last year Nancy moved to part-time status in our mailroom three months before she was to move across the United States. During this time I conducted the performance reviews for all of the full-time team members, but not for Nancy. When I came into the office over the next few weeks, I could tell something was wrong. No one said anything, but I could tell there was a problem. Then one day Nancy knocked on my door and asked if she could talk to me. I welcomed her, and she walked in with tears running down her cheeks. I asked her what was wrong. She looked up and asked, 'Don't you care about me any more? You didn't give me a performance review? Aren't you interested in my growth after I leave here?' Well, of course I cared; and she was in the right. From that day on, all employees, full- or part-time, paid or unpaid, were included in the performance review programme. It is an investment in their growth and an important way for the organization and the leader to say, 'I care.'

Performance reviews are about caring enough to commit yourself to assisting people to do the best job possible. If the work is not up to standard, this is the time to help the person bring it up or, if that is not possible, to help the employee or volunteer relocate where their gifts can be better used. If it is about caring, then it belongs in every leadership relationship. If it is about focus on the mission, then it belongs in every leadership relationship. Every member of the organization, every volunteer – paid and unpaid – is owed a performance review as the organization's minimal investment in their growth and development.

Obviously the heart of the review process is not the particular form or model chosen. It is the discussion that follows, the relationship between the leader and the follower, and the action regarding, 'Where do we go from here?' In fact, it is dangerous to adopt any form that might distract from the relationship, the discussion and the personal investment of the leader in the employee.

Performance reviews are most effective when they are part of a leadership relationship of continuous feedback. People deserve to know how they are doing all the time, to be able to get the feedback they need when they need it in order to improve and do their job well. Annual feedback is not sufficient. It is too far removed from the moment. To have learning value, feedback needs to be immediate, while the person can still do something about it. If we care about followers and their growth, we will tell them what they are doing wrong now so they can correct it. Or we tell them what they are doing well now so they can keep at it. In fact, I believe that feedback given long after the fact is more a sign of not caring than of true leadership responsibility. I believe that if the leader does not point out problems along the way so that followers can correct their actions, then he or she loses the right to do so at the annual review.

In the 80s, the best-selling little book *The One Minute Manager*[6] argued persuasively for continuous review and appraisal, suggesting regular one-minute praises and one-minute reprimands. I agree completely with the principle of continuous feedback that the authors advocated. The technique proposed, however, was a little mechanical, prompting another book, the *Fifty-nine Second Employee: How to Stay One Second ahead of Your One-Minute Manager!*[7] I do not want to argue for a particular technique here but for a principle of relationship – regular conversation and discussion, continuous feedback and learning.

I want the people for whose success I am responsible to know exactly how they are doing before the annual performance review. We conduct our performance reviews at Regent College during May and June using the model I will outline here. We have been using this model since I arrived at Regent in 1988. When I was at Fuller Seminary, I developed the approach that we called the continuous review model. It was one of three models available to managers. The other two were more traditional annual review forms – assessment checklists. We used my model in my department of the seminary. At Regent we set up this model as the institutional model. (There are some privileges to being president!) When I arrived at Regent, I found the usual reluctance to conduct performance reviews. Most managers and employees had had enough bad experiences to resist re-establishing this 'demeaning and discouraging' element in our management process. After taking the leadership team through a performance review process, I think they found it reasonably painless, if not helpful, and they then applied the model to their people. We now have the model operational so that, I hope, employees are getting continuous feedback about their work and that they find the performance review time an opportunity for self-assessment and a time to give feedback to the leadership regarding how we could better support them in their contribution and growth.

In our model, I provide a list of questions to the person being reviewed about a week before the scheduled meeting. I have eight questions for the management team for whom I am responsible. A similar set of nine questions is used for the team members without management responsibilities. Each person is expected to come to their interview prepared to speak to these questions.

Before I conduct a performance review, I write a personal letter of thanks to the person, expressing my appreciation for the contribution he or she has made this past year. If we have been working on a problem area, I might allude to that in the letter, but basically it is a letter of affirmation and thanks. I hand that letter to the person at the beginning of the interview. Then I listen.

The interview lasts about one hour. For most of that time, the manager being reviewed assesses his or her own contribution by discussing the answers to the eight questions set out below. I take notes. The questions reveal the direction of this performance review conversation:

1. **How do you evaluate your contribution to Regent College this past year?**
   This is a time for the manager to assess and evaluate his or

her strengths, weaknesses and contributions to the college. Such self-assessment is much more effective at highlighting areas for needed growth than the leader's assessment. Hardly ever have I had a person give a completely biased evaluation of themselves that I needed to correct. If we have had an honest relationship throughout the year, their evaluation will be fairly honest and perhaps more vulnerable.

2. **How do you evaluate Regent's relationship to you? Has the college lived up to your expectations?**
   This gives the manager a chance to assess how well they have fitted into the team, how well the college has delivered on its promises. This question can be difficult for the leader because it invites managers to let us know when we have not fulfilled their expectations. There are times when I have had to agree and apologize when a manager pointed out that that year I had been so preoccupied with my work that I had not been there for the manager as much as he or she needed. In many ways this form of review puts the follower into the role of reviewer.

3. **How have the members of your team grown under your leadership?**
   This is a question that the board puts to me. It is a reminder for managers that their work is measured most by the growth of their people. This gives them the opportunity to articulate how they have invested in their people and how they have measured the results.

4. **What do you see as your primary objectives for this coming year?**
   Here the person presents the first draft of annual key objectives for discussion. The conversation will focus on content, implementation and the support or assistance needed from me.

5. **What elements make you excited about your work next year?**
   Here I want to tap into their vision – to get them to articulate the vision that drives them into the new year. It is

easy for routine jobs to get old – for people to stop growing. Most people need something new and fresh to keep their interest. This is what we talked about under vision. I want them to talk about their vision for Regent and their contribution to that vision.

6. **What could you not do next year without harming our ability to achieve our mission?**
Peter Drucker calls this sloughing off the old. We cannot keep adding new things to do without creating space, by getting rid of some things that we no longer need to do. This does not come naturally to most of us in leadership. This question is designed to get us thinking. What could we stop doing to make space to try something new?

7. **What kind of training or continuing education pro-gramme have you planned for next year?**
I assume that all managers at Regent will be engaged in some form of training to learn their job more effectively or in continuing education to prepare them for increased responsibilities. I want them to think about this before the meeting and come with a proposal for their own personal development. In some cases where we have promoted a person to a new level without experience, we will build the training into the compensation package. A few years ago Mary Lam, our financial manager, became the chief administrative officer of the college. As part of the increased compensation package that goes with the posi-tion, we gave her a sum of money for attendance at pro-fessional training events that target her new responsibilities. During the first year, we also set aside funds that she could draw on to bring in consultants to advise her in areas where her experience had not yet caught up with her responsibilities.

8. **What can I do to support your growth in the job, in your ministry, in your career?**
This is the point where I make myself available as their servant. How do I help them grow? Sometimes it means getting out of their way. Sometimes it means being more

available. Sometimes it means just caring and praying as someone is struggling to make a strategic decision about their life.

This final question also brings us back to the key element of leadership. Leadership is a relationship. It is an investment of one person in another, to influence their thoughts, beliefs, actions and behaviours. It is a relationship in which both the leader and the follower should grow. I have used this model of performance reviews for over 15 years with full-time and part-time employees, paid and unpaid. I have found it to be an affirming and motivating model. It is forward looking rather than giving a grade for past actions. When I presented the model at the University of Calgary's Executive Management Program, the faculty member responsible for personnel development liked it but suggested I call it Performance (P)review, because it is driven more by tomorrow than yesterday. I like that.

The questions for persons without management responsibility are similar:

1. How do you evaluate your contribution to Regent College this past year? Do you believe you have learned the job? Do you feel like part of the team?

2. Have we fulfilled our promises? Have we fulfilled your expectations?

3. Look at your job description. Do you think it is accurate when compared to what you actually did this year?
   With this question we bring the job description back into focus for review. If there is no discrepancy between the description and the experience, we are probably on target. If there is a difference, either the job description needs rewriting to be more accurate or the work assignments need to be adjusted to meet the design of the position. This question again sees the job in terms of its contribution to mission.

4. (optional) How do you assess your progress on the issues we have been seeking to correct?

5. (optional) What objectives do we need to set for these areas? With what set review time?
   Questions 4 and 5 allow for the possibility that some negative feedback has been given during the year and a plan is being worked on to correct the problem. The annual review should not ignore that problem, but should look at it again, measure progress and set a time frame for action and further review.

6. **What do you want to do next year to make your job more interesting, more responsible?**
   This looks for individual vision. While not every proposal that emerges from every employee can be implemented, we have received some very good ideas from the people who are deep in the trenches.

7. **What could you not do next year without harming our ability to achieve our mission?**

8. **What do we agree should be your specific objectives for next year?**

9. **What can I do this year to help you move towards your goals in this office, in your personal ministry and career path?**

When the interview is over, I place a copy of my notes and anything the employee gave me in writing in that person's file. If the discussion dealt with anything controversial or negative related to their work, I summarize the discussion in writing and send the person a copy before I file it. Again, we have found this model to be very effective at strengthening the relationship between the leader and the follower and keeping us working together as a team with shared vision and shared values in pursuit of a shared mission.

Equip for performance and growth

The final principle of people development focuses on providing the training and continuing education needed for followers to grow in their positions. If the performance review seeks to develop the employee or volunteer by preparing them for more responsibility, then it should result in some action for that development, supported by additional education. We have tried to build this into our managerial review, but it should probably be included in the staff review as well for I expect every person at Regent College to be learning and growing.

Leaders should think of every person for whose success they are responsible as someone they are training for a better position, for an expanded ministry. What kind of training does that person need? How can we keep their commitment high? How can we improve their ability to serve the kingdom of God? I want to believe that every person who accepts employment at Regent, paid or unpaid, will leave the college better equipped for service and ministry than when they arrived. It is part of our investment in the resources that God places in our care.

Leadership is an empowering, individual relationship. *An individual leader* – you or me, with all of our own cultural baggage and experiences, coming with our own level of maturity at that moment and frequently bringing a preconceived idea of the appropriate style of leadership – *in a caring relationship* – that takes the other person seriously and builds trust, cares for the development and growth of the other person and seeks to empower that person to accomplish his or her task for the mission of the organization to the glory of God – *with an individual follower* – a person with his or her own cultural baggage and experiences, coming with a preconceived idea of the appropriate style of leadership that the leader should exercise – *at a particular level of maturity* – a competence and confidence that varies from day to day and frequently within the same day – *in a specific situation* – right now, today, this task, in these conditions. Effective leaders are engaged in such empowering relationships with the people for whom they are responsible that the appropriate leadership style is an adapted response to CAREing for each person in the shared pursuit of vision, values and service.

Conclusion: Leadership Is the Use of Power to Serve the People

To conclude this chapter we will turn to another biblical vignette that underscores the role of leadership in the care and nurture of the people whom God entrusts to us and reminds us of our accountability before God, which is the theme of the final chapter.

They were the political rulers and spiritual leaders of a mighty nation, a country blessed by God. They led a nation whose armed forces were respected beyond their relative size on the international scene. This was a country founded on high religious principles, one nation, living under God. A blessed country with natural and native resources, strategically positioned for strong international trade. The human, natural and spiritual potential for leadership on the world's stage was great.

And yet these leaders were deposed from their offices. The political leaders fell to internal coups or were defeated in war. The religious leaders were written off as irrelevant to a modern people. The form of their piety and the skill of their rhetoric were applauded, but they made no difference in the lives and behaviours of those around them (Ezek. 30:30–33). Why?

One man stood up and told them why – a preacher named Ezekiel. After the nation of Judah was defeated by Babylon, Jerusalem, its capital, was destroyed and the people exiled to other countries, Ezekiel, a prophet and priest living under the authority of his God, addressed the political and religious leaders with a message from God. Listen to the words of Ezekiel:

> The word of the Lord came to me: 'Son of man, prophesy against the shepherds of Israel; prophesy and say to them: "This is what the Sovereign Lord says: Woe to the shepherds of Israel who only take care of themselves! Should not shepherds take care of the flock? You eat the curds, clothe yourselves with the wool and slaughter the choice animals, but you do not take care of the flock. You have not strengthened the weak or healed the

sick or bound up the injured. You have not brought back the strays or searched for the lost. You have ruled them harshly and brutally. So they were scattered because there was no shepherd, and when they were scattered they became food for all the wild animals. My sheep wandered over all the mountains and on every high hill. They were scattered over the whole earth, and no one searched or looked for them.

"Therefore, you shepherds, hear the word of the Lord: As surely as I live, declares the Sovereign Lord, because my flock lacks a shepherd and so has been plundered and has become food for all the wild animals, and because my shepherds did not search for my flock but cared for themselves rather than for my flock, therefore, O shepherds, hear the word of the Lord: This is what the Sovereign Lord says: I am against the shepherds and will hold them accountable for my flock. I will remove them from tending the flock so that the shepherds can no longer feed themselves. I will rescue my flock from their mouths, and it will no longer be food for them.'" (Ezek. 34:1–10)

The political and religious leaders of Israel had used their power – the positions and resources that God had given them and their country – for their own benefit, their own gain. They had grown fat off the flock but they had not used their power and authority to feed the flock, to care for and nurture the people for whom they were responsible.

We have been given an awesome responsibility – to feed the sheep of God, to care for the people of God. We are accountable to God for the use of the power he has given us. The prophets are watching. How will we use our power?

Notes

[1] Max DePree, *Leadership is an Art* (East Lansing: Michigan State University Press, 1987), 27; see also Max DePree, *Leading Without Power* (San Francisco: Jossey-Bass, 1997).
[2] *Fast Company: How Smart Business Works*, August 1998.
[3] *The Vancouver Sun*, July 1990.
[4] Scott Kirsner, 'Hire Today ... Gone Tomorrow', *Fast Company*, August 1998, 138.

[5] Peters and Austin, *Passion*, 213–218.
[6] Kenneth H. Blanchard and Spencer Johnson, *The One Minute Manager* (New York: Morrow, 1982).
[7] Rae Andre and Peter Ward, *Fifty-nine Second Employee* (Boston: Houghton-Mifflin, 1983).

Chapter VI

Influencing with Accountability

Accountability: Patience and Perseverance

With the words of Ezekiel that ended the last chapter still ringing in our ears, we come to this final chapter, looking again to Jude, the half-brother of our Lord, for an image with which to launch these concluding thoughts on relational leadership. The fifth and final image that Jude used of those false leaders who were exerting influence in his community is both graphic and sobering: 'Wandering stars, for whom blackest darkness has been reserved.' A flash of excitement streaking across life's stage, swallowed up without performance. No commitment, no patience or perseverance, no long-term investment in the people – nothing to show that leadership was ever there. A burst of energy that calls attention to the leader but makes no lasting difference.

Unlike the previous images, this one carries within it its own judgement. Shooting stars, swallowed up in the darkness of the sky, capture well the shallow and temporary charisma of leaders who disappear from the scene before having any significant impact on the people or the mission. They are on their own journey and are not leaders caring for the people. Note the negative ending of this image. Jude does not simply say 'swallowed up in darkness'. He puts a judgemental twist to it. They are people 'for whom blackest darkness has been reserved'. They are accountable! They do not just disappear. Darkness is their place. They are swallowed up in darkness precisely because they shine only for themselves. They have nothing to offer the people. They leave nothing of substance behind.

Paul and Philemon: a Relationship of Accountability

One last time we return briefly to our story of Philemon and his important relationship with Paul. Paul is not a flash in the dark. His faith has been called to account. He sits in prison for his love of Christ and his love of people. He has invested his life in the people that God has placed him among and continues to do so, even under arrest. He is in prison because of servant leadership, because he chose to serve the resurrected Christ and the people of God.

And Paul wants to make sure that Philemon also is not all talk and charisma. Paul wants action, he wants Philemon's faith to make a difference. He expects Philemon to practise what he preaches – to live up to Paul's expectations. Paul holds Philemon accountable. Paul is saying to Philemon, 'Remember all those sermons and speeches about community? Remember those lessons on forgiveness and reconciliation? Well, it is time to demonstrate that you really believe what you proclaim! Reinstate Onesimus into your home and embrace him as a brother in Christ.' This powerful little letter with its agenda of influence is about accountability.

And there is more. The letter calls Philemon to account, to live out his values, his beliefs. But Paul adds one more layer of accountability, 'And one thing more: Prepare a guest room for me, because I hope to be restored to you in answer to your prayers.' In other words, I intend to visit and confirm that you have in fact been reconciled with Onesimus. That is accountability. There will be a performance review.

For Jude and for Paul, leaders are accountable. The servant leader commits to the people and pursues a purpose. Leadership makes a difference; it should make a lasting difference. Relational leaders are accountable for their personal contribution to the common mission and the growth of the people for whose contribution they are responsible. They are also accountable for their own continued personal growth.

Accountability and Vulnerability

In this concluding chapter I want to look at the accountability and vulnerability of the relational leader. We have been entrusted by God with an awesome responsibility – the care and nurture of his people. We have been given the task of leadership – an audacious undertaking. We know that we are frail human vessels, weak and easily distracted. We need the discipline of accountability to keep us focused on our responsibilities before God. We will look at accountability to God, accountability to the organization and accountability for ourselves.

Because we are accountable, we are vulnerable. It is a risk to lead, a risk to enter into a relationship of interdependency with another person, a risk to offer ourselves in service to a mission and to people. The possibility of failure is high and often outside of our control. Leadership is about accountability and vulnerability. But if leadership is so accountable, why take the risk? Why accept such vulnerability? The only reason I can think of to accept leadership responsibility is because God asks us to and offers us as a gift to his people (Rom. 12). And if we lead because God has asked, we have confidence that our vulnerability is wrapped in the hope of forgiveness. Relational leadership – servant leadership – is also about forgiveness.

Accountability to God

This theme has been touched on throughout this study. We are in this business because God has called us to serve. And we know that our impact upon ministry is directly related to our dependence upon God. We cannot do it alone. We will have the kind of impact that Jude and Paul are expecting only if the power of God works in and through us. We need the continual renewing presence of Christ beside us as we undertake the daunting task of leadership.

Accountability to God is about personal renewal and dependence. I cannot offer a stock formula for our personal development before God. Each of us works out the pattern that is best for us. But I do want to call us back to the resources for leadership that we noted at the end of Jude's letter. In particular I want to underline the importance of Scripture and prayer – listening to God.

I have always tried to maintain some kind of ongoing personal relationship with God, some kind of devotional time built into my days, my week. However, it has not always been easy to find a constant and successful model. I hate getting up early in the morning, and I am too tired at night. Once the day is under way, my mind is captive to the full agenda that calls for my time. I have always had the freedom of continuous informal conversation or prayer with God, but I have not always been successful at setting aside a specific time for listening and talking to God. At least until now! When I took on the responsibilities of leadership at Regent College, I knew I was in over my head. I had never been a president before and was not sure I was capable of the task. I felt the awesome responsibility of the mission and the community that God was entrusting to my leadership. From the day I arrived in Vancouver, I found that time to be with God came much more easily. It came out of dependence and fear of failure! I knew that I could not do this job without the constant presence and power of God. I could not imagine starting a day of responsibilities without first praying through the day with God and seeking to understand what was at stake. This complete sense of dependence and need drove me to take the time to pray for those for whom I was responsible, to pray for wisdom, vision and energy as I thought through the agenda for the day.

Now, eleven years later, this has become a fixed part of my day. I begin each morning with time in Scripture and prayer, trying to listen to God and understand what is important about the day ahead. For me at least, I have come to realize that there is a direct correlation between being 'in over my head' and finding time to spend with God. When I think I have my job under control, it is easier to skip the devotional meditative time with God. But when I am aware of my vulnerability, my complete dependence, that time becomes a priority. So much so that I realize that the reverse of this observation is also true. When I am not spending consistent time with God, it probably means that I am not taking much of a risk in my faith. I believe there is a correlation between recognizing your dependence upon God and investing time in listening to God. Obviously I still believe that I am in over my head in my current responsibilities!

In this context, prayer is an important part of my listening to God. I find that it is often during times of prayer that my mind sees the reality of my day from a different perspective. I keep paper and pencil with my Bible and allow myself to stop and write down ideas that come during prayer and reading. I am convinced that the meditative mind works differently from the reasoning mind. I see and think differently during times of prayer and meditation. This has become a significant inspirational time for me. I get many of my leadership ideas, sermon outlines and relational convictions while reading Scripture and praying. While I do lift up others in intercession and place my own agenda before God, I have found these times to be much more times of listening and seeing things from God's perspective.

By definition leaders occupy a risky position. We are responsible for decisions that affect the lives and work of others as well as ourselves. Leadership decisions have to be made because we do not know what the right decision is. It does not take much leadership to choose the obviously right answer. In fact, some would define leadership as the task of making a decision when the alternatives are equal. The *risk* of choosing when the right choice is uncertain is part of what drives me to prayer.

As a middle manager, I could recommend decisions, knowing that 'someone wiser' with responsibility for me would correct or modify my decisions if I was wrong. Now as president there is no one providing that layer of protection. Thus, my dependence upon God becomes more crucial. Every morning I pray through my agenda for the day. During the day I pray for wisdom to see things from God's perspective, to look through the eyes of Jesus and understand what is important here, what issues are at stake. In the evening, frequently at the instigation of my wife, I review the day, giving thanks to God for what he has done in our midst. Prayer for me is more an expression of my weakness and dependence than an expectation that God will make the decision for me. I think prayer brings us into the mind of God so that we understand what is important, what are the values that must be preserved. Occasionally I get brilliant insights when asking for such wisdom, but usually just a reinforcement of the values that are at issue. My prayer as a leader is that I will do no harm and my final confidence lies in the belief that I cannot frustrate the sovereign will of God.

Listening to God is foundational. This priority for Christian leaders has been a primary assumption of this study: *Build in time for your spiritual growth.* Incorporate worship and nurture. Allow time alone. Build in time with God. Find your Sabbath rhythm, that devotional space, where you stop to let your soul catch up with your body. Take time to be with God, not just study God. Leadership is a relationship of service. As Jude reminds us, it begins in relationship with God and leads out of the strength of that relationship.

Accountability to the organization

There are two things I want to mention here: Self-assessment and renewal, and working with a board. A good board will hold you accountable to the mission and the people and expect you to participate in some form of review and evaluation. But as leaders we should be engaged in an on-going self-assessment of our leadership and growth, including maintaining an appropriate balance of commitments to life outside of our organization.

1. Self-assessment and performance review

When I accepted the role of president at Regent, I asked the board for an annual performance review. I want to know regularly how I am doing. Am I living up to their expectations? What kind of leadership will the college need in five or ten years? Can I be equipped for that role? It is an opportunity for the college to hold me accountable to the mission and the community and for me to hold the college accountable for their investment in me.

The initiation of this process each year normally comes from the chairperson of the board or from me. At an agreed-upon time, I draft a five- to ten-page self-assessment of my contribution to the college. I try to be honest, reviewing the positive accomplishments and the negative results. I review my strengths and growth, and I admit my weaknesses and disappointments. I evaluate the growth and progress of those for whose success I am responsible. I assess the relationship between the president and the board. And I outline what I am doing for my own growth and renewal. I also highlight the key objectives for the year ahead. This evaluation is sent to the chairperson who appoints a small committee of board members to review my performance. Normally I will meet with them for three to four hours, discussing our relationship. These have been important times – not always easy, but necessary for the continued development of the relationship between the president and the board and the continued growth of both.

Continued learning and growth is critical for leaders. We serve changing organizations in a changing world. The demands on leadership time far exceed the time we have to give. We can easily become so busy leading and serving that we do not take the time for renewal and growth. Study, learning and continual renewal are crucial to leadership. It is hard to sustain vision when we are tired. It is difficult to lead when we are not growing. New learning is empowering. It is renewing, and creates the energy needed for leadership. That is why we build continuing education into the performance review and assessment process. Leaders must carve out time for their own learning and growth even as they expect it of the people they lead.

As I noted above, the performance review is an instrument for growth and leadership development. The purpose of my review is to equip me to be the kind of leader that Regent needs as we move into the years ahead. The board and I want to be the most effective leadership team we can be, carrying out the trust that God has placed in our hands.

2. Boards

That brings us to the topic of boards. There is probably no more important and potentially problematic relationship in leadership than the relationship between the leader and the governing board. We cannot begin to do this topic justice in the space available, but I do want to raise it for further thought.

In non-profit organizations or, as Drucker calls it, the service sector, leaders are held accountable to their people, to the mission and to the broader society by volunteer boards of trustees, governors or directors. The board is the governing body entrusted with the mission. It is responsible for the ongoing vitality and health of the organization or church as it pursues its mission. The board holds the mission and the resources in trust and thinks strategically about the future development of the organization. The board is responsible for selecting the people to whom they will delegate the leadership of the organization and for holding the leaders accountable to live out the vision and values of the community. Boards provide strategic thinking but not day-to-day management.

Leaders must invest in the development of strong and knowledgeable boards who understand the mission and take ownership of the vision and resources. This is a major responsibility for those of us who provide leadership in the 'service' or ministry sector. And yet this is a major point of tension for many organizations precisely because it creates two sets of 'owners', two complementary and competing points of leadership: the appointed leader and the governing board. Both are responsible, both are vitally invested, both are 'owners', both have vision. The board normally has final authority, but the leader frequently has more time invested and more knowledge about the life of the organization. Working together, boards and leaders provide a powerful team for leadership. Working against each other, they create a nightmare for the organization. On average, college and seminary presidents change every four years. Hospital administrators have similarly short terms. When tensions emerge, the leader leaves. Pastors often have the opposite problem. When tensions emerge, the board members leave or the board is marginalized. Too many pastors ignore the board and try to run the church on their own.

I do not have the answer for this struggle. I think it is endemic to our kind of organizations. But I still believe in the model. Leaders need accountability to keep them focused. The board is the primary agent for this accountability in our kind of community. We need to strengthen the board, to invest in their growth and knowledge, to create lines of communication that encourage the shared leadership that must emerge. Leaders without accountability to the people and the mission, without a structure to keep them focused, are in great danger of misusing power for their own benefit. Dietrich Bonhoeffer's prophetic radio message when Hitler came to power underscores the dangerous tension between exercising leadership, accountable to the people and being the leader, *Der Führer*, accountable to oneself.[1] The board is the primary accountability relationship for the leader in a church or non-profit organization. We need strong boards.

While the board is necessary, it must learn the difference between its responsibilities and those of the leadership team. The board must delegate leadership and step back, monitoring strategically. It must give its trust to the leadership and be available as needed for expertise and advice to the leadership. The board must learn to exercise responsibility without managing. The leadership must learn to be open and accountable without undercutting the board's responsibility. We are talking about *shared leadership, accountability and trust*. It is a partnership of shared vision. Leaders can only lead accountably when they are given responsibility and assessed regularly in light of the mission and values of the community.

There is much more that could be said about boards. Books have been written on this subject. But for the purpose of this study, suffice it to say that they are a critically important element of accountability in our organizations, an element that needs work and development as we seek ways to provide the kind of leadership our organizations will need in the 21st century.

Accountability for ourselves

Two topics need to be touched on here: understanding time and getting a life. Over the years, 'time management' has been one of the two most requested workshops I lead. (The 'leadership of volunteers' is the other.) Leaders struggle with time. There is not enough. It seems to get away from us. Yet we are accountable. We are responsible for our use of time and, often, for other people's use of time. It is important that leaders understand time – understand that there are different ways to view time and that leaders and followers may have different perspectives on the time they share. It is also important that they find balance in their investment of time. This study is about the leadership relationship. That is the focus of attention for servant leaders. But it is not enough. We owe our organizations a larger life. Leaders need vital and nurturing relationships outside of the organization to enrich their thinking and broaden their perspective on life. Two in particular deserve mention here: family and friends.

1. Understanding time
Whenever I am asked to talk about managing time, setting priorities and living with commitments, I am always a little ambivalent. I am a serious believer in time management, in setting priorities, in articulating values and in keeping commitments. Accountability for the management of our time is a problem that plagues us all. We all have a problem managing our time. There is never enough time! Yet there is very little I can say here that you have not already heard before or do not already know. The problem is *not* knowing *how* to manage your time. The problem is *doing it!* We do not like to discipline ourselves. Most leaders have very loose accountability for the use of time. In fact, many times we deliberately choose to manage our time poorly to avoid something. It is also hard to talk about time management without being reminded how poorly I manage my own time! Time management is about being accountable for ourselves. It is about managing our lives before God – being stewards of our time.

Time is a fleeting resource slipping through our fingers, like sand in an hourglass ... *or is it?* That brings up another problem in the management of time. People see time differently depending on the culture in which they were raised and the personal assumptions that have formed in them over the years.

Researchers tend to identify two basic views of time: monochronic time and polychronic time.[2] But I do not need the research to know that there are different views of time. I have been married to Beverly for thirty-six years! That is enough to convince me! You cannot get more divergent views of time than the views that Beverly and I have. I set my watch with precision wanting to know exactly where I am on the world's time continuum. Beverly does not like to wear a watch, and when she does she deliberately sets it 5 to 15 minutes off – she can't remember how much! – so it cannot control her life. You can imagine the many points of conflict that occur like 'clockwork' in our relationship. People see time differently depending on their culture, their education, their style of thinking, their logic or creativity.

Monochronic time – is seen as linear, incremental, sequential and predictable. The focus is on goals, objectives, deadlines. Time is seen as a resource to be expended. There is a tendency to focus and narrow our thinking, to do one thing at a time.[3]

Polychronic time – is seen as layered, almost spatial. It is normal to be multitasking, doing many things at once without regard to a linear passing of time. The focus is on values and relationships. Because many things are going on simultaneously, it is not unusual for a person to diverge off, in and out of various tasks, with no visible logic to the pattern – at least from the perspective of monochronic time.[4]

I believe we live in a world that requires us to draw on both views of time. Yet our starting point is influenced by the culture we were raised in, by our style of thinking, by our left-brain–right-brain mix. These are not hard and fast categories but more like overlapping tendencies.

In general, Western cultures like that in North America value monochronic time more highly than polychronic, while Latin, Asian and African cultures tend to value polychronic time more highly.[5]

Within both sets of cultures, however, we find people who tend towards convergent thinking – focusing and concentrating – and people who tend towards divergent thinking – looking at the big picture. People whose style of thinking is more convergent, more focused and concentrated, tend to be more comfortable in monochronic time. People whose style of thinking is more divergent, looking at the big picture, tend to be more comfortable in polychronic time. Similarly, research suggests that left-brain people who prefer structure and logic move towards monochronic time, while right-brain people who prefer creativity and spontaneity move towards polychronic time.[6]

Why do I bother with any of this? Because I believe that we need both views of time to carry out the responsibilities of leadership by serving as relational leaders in our Christian communities. Also, in most of our organizations we serve a community that incorporates a variety of approaches to time. At Regent College in any given year about half of the community will be more comfortable with monochronic time and about half will look at time as polychronic. We have differences – and that's OK. That is what community is all about. We cannot expect the person sitting next to us to view time the same way we do. But we should take the opportunity to learn what others see because we must cultivate both perspectives.

One quick illustration from the world of education. If monochronic time draws on time frames and deadlines, it is clear that education is basically monochronic. Students have nine months to complete the academic year. They have identifiable amounts of reading, papers to write and deadlines when those papers are due. Regardless of their culture or orientation, they are undertaking a programme of study that operates in monochronic time. The polychronic people must adjust to that reality. At the same time, we stress community at Regent College. Community cannot be programmed. Twenty minutes a day given to relationship building does not necessarily build friendships. Community building and the nurture of relationships are polychronic. They cannot be scheduled. The monochronic people must adjust to that reality. We live in a world that requires us to blend our approaches to time. But because we believe in community, we can learn from one another.

We can see how this fits with our leadership agenda. Leaders are responsible for leading an organization and nurturing a community – two sides of the same coin for these are the same people. Leaders are responsible for vision and values. We translate our vision into action by monochronic thinking, by focusing our energy and concentrating the resources of the organization on our mission. Our planning processes are a monochronic, linear way of looking at our organization. Yet we are also responsible for the values system. Leaders reinforce the values and culture of the organization. This calls for polychronic thinking, involving creativity, divergent thinking and a holistic look at the big picture of who we are and what is important to us. Leaders must be able to work with both. Mission achievement requires a monochronic approach to time; community building requires a polychronic approach. Neither is right; neither is wrong. They are two ways of looking at who we are and what is important. But it is critical for us to remember that most of us are more comfortable with one approach than the other. It is important that we know ourselves, that we understand which approach to time we find most appealing. We will need partners in our organization who work comfortably with the other approach. Together, in community, we can provide the leadership our organizations need in these times of rapid change.

2. Getting a life

The demands of organizational leadership can consume one. Supporting the network of relationships that make up an organizational community is a never-ending assignment. Leaders are vulnerable to burn-out when they let the organization become their life, and organizations can consume any leader. There is more to be done in any organization than any

leader can possibly do in one life. That is why we have shared
vision, shared values, teams and delegation. But we owe our
organizations more than that. We owe them a life. Leaders
need commitments and relationships outside of the organization to give them perspective and energy – to enable them to
bring something to share with the organization. We have
looked at the leader's relationship with God. There are also
the relationships of family and friends. Leaders owe it to
themselves to keep balance in their lives, to invest themselves
in these critical relationships outside of the organization.
They owe it to their family and friends. And they owe it to
the organization. Leaders must get a life if they want to bring
life to their organization.

(1) Family commitments: I have very strong feelings about
family commitments. They are a top priority for me. I believe
that if you have chosen to marry, you have made a lifetime
commitment to the well-being and growth of your spouse.
That becomes a very high priority. Graduate students have a
notorious track record of shattered marriages because they
spend all their time in the library and ignore their spouses.
Theological students can be worse because they are 'doing it
for God'. Patterns set early in our lives and study will shape
our priorities for leadership. Too many families fall apart in
the circles of Christian leadership because the leaders are so
busy serving God that they fail to attend to their families.
This is inexcusable. Get a life! Leaders need to balance their
commitment to relationships. If we have entered into the
commitment of marriage, we have been given and accepted a
priority field for ministry. If we cannot minister intentionally
and effectively at home, I have serious questions about our
ministry anywhere! Beverly and I have struggled with time
and many other things over the years, but our relationship
has been a top priority for both of us. That has meant investing the time to communicate. In addition to all of the normal
time spent together over meals, in the car, at church, we
usually spend a minimum of an hour every day in face-to-
face talking and listening, without doing anything else. It
takes time to nurture a relationship!

We did the same with our two sons. From the time the older was five until the younger left for university, over and above all of the normal family time, I took one of them out for dinner every Wednesday evening, just to talk about them with them. For sixteen years! I still enjoy their company, and they still like to have me buy dinner. Think about it. How much quality face-to-face time do you spend each day talking and listening to the members of your family?

(2) Friends: Leaders need *friends* – men and women outside of the organization with whom we enjoy life, with whom we learn things not related to the organizational mission, with whom we discover new things and grow in our walk with God. Friends add to the maturity that a leader brings to the organization. Friendships should be a priority for any leader.

One winter Beverly and I were vacationing on the beach in Mexico. We watched three men in their seventies laughing and talking, swimming and bantering. Their wives were sitting up in the shade. As I watched them, I found myself thinking about the later years of my life. Would I have three friends with whom to swim on the beach or to hike in the mountains? I realized that if this was going to be important to me then, I would need to keep investing in those relationships now. We do not attain that level of friendship without a lifetime of relationship! Leaders cannot allow their organizational responsibilities to so narrow their focus that they fail to invest in the broader network of friends in the various communities in which God has placed them.

This remains another priority for both Beverly and me. We have committed ourselves to small support groups that have met weekly for the past twenty-nine years. And we stay in touch with many of those in whom we have made such an investment. The Beckers in New Mexico, the Partens in Minneapolis, the Whites in Los Angeles, and others that I could name – people with whom we pick up a conversation in mid-sentence even after lengthy absence and geographical distance.

And then there is my mountaineering group. Don Bosch, Brent Stenberg, Rich Butman, Don Dwyer, Newt Malony, Steve Sittig and I have been climbing mountains, sleeping in snow caves and canoeing rivers together now for nearly twenty-five years. We went on our first hike together on Thanksgiving weekend in 1975 and have taken at least three trips together every year since. Not only do we enjoy sharing the wilderness together, but over the years we have come to realize that these are important relationships – six other men that we trust with our lives – men with whom we have shared nearly twenty-five years of life and personal growth as well as wilderness trips. This is friendship. They are people who know me thoroughly and like me anyway! They provide balance and perspective outside of the pressure of organizational responsibilities. There is nothing we cannot talk about, nothing we do not talk about. They come from different worlds, have different responsibilities. They greatly enrich my life. We get together as much for the relationships now as we do for the mountain climbing. This has become an important priority for me. I build into my life time to climb mountains with these friends, time to call them and see how they are doing. I plan trips through Los Angeles, Memphis and Chicago, and they come to Vancouver. We want to be doing this together when we hit eighty, and we are making the investment in that future now!

These are polychronic commitments. We cannot make relationships happen in our time frame, but we can build friendships into our priorities and make sure that we save time for the people in our lives. Twenty years from now, the relationships we have formed will be more important than the achievements of our leadership. Being accountable for my time means making time for friendships that reach beyond the borders of leadership responsibilities; it means finding a balance between leadership relationships and life relationships.

Accountability and Forgiveness

Leaders hold followers accountable to the organizational mission and their own contribution and growth. Boards hold leaders accountable in the same way. But leaders and

followers alike are accountable to God, to one another and
to the mission that brings them into relationship. *Leadership
is an interdependent relationship of accountability, grounded
in a relationship with God in Christ.* It is the final clause of
this sentence that gives us hope. Leadership is accountable.
Relational leadership is vulnerable. In relationship with God,
because of Christ, we have hope. When God calls us to leadership – when God calls us to life – that call includes forgiveness. I do not believe there can be leadership without
forgiveness.

In the spring of 1996, tragedy struck the world of mountaineering. Two leaders lost their lives. On May 10, Rob Hall
and Scott Fischer died in the pursuit of their vision. So did
six other men and women in one of the worst climbing disasters in Mount Everest's history. You may have seen it
reported in the news, read the painful article in *Outside* magazine, seen the television special 'Mountain Without Mercy'
or seen the IMAX production of 'Everest'.

Mountains don't forgive. This principle has long been part
of the lore and literature of mountaineering. People make
mistakes, people can forgive. But mountains are not a forgiving environment. We all know this; climbers know it very
well. But we still react with shock and outrage when it
happens. The margin for error is very slim at 29,000 feet, but
we still scream with pain when the price of a decision is
death!

No one knows exactly what went wrong on May 10.
There has been much speculation and there will be more as
climbers, sponsors, families and spectators reflect on the
Everest tragedy. For some it was an error of vision. No one
in their right mind would undertake such an objective, let
alone pay $65,000 for the opportunity! For some it was an
error of values. The interdependent community of climbers
caring for one another was replaced by a collection of individual egos pursuing their own dreams. For some it was an
act of God as a beautiful morning deteriorated into a hellish
hurricane of freezing wind and snow. For many, however, it
all boils down to an error of leadership. Leadership at multiple levels. Governmental leadership that failed to control the

number of climbers attempting to ascend. Organizational leadership that allowed expeditions to compete rather than cooperate, putting twenty-three climbers in each other's way on the final push to the summit. And individual leadership that allowed personal aspirations to set aside the rules of the climb. Mistakes were made and mountains are not forgiving.

Rob Hall was a seasoned leader, an experienced guide who organized and led commercial climbs to the top of the world. Widely respected, he was known as a solid and conservative leader, a good man to climb with. He was a leader that people chose to follow. He understood leadership as a relationship of trust. He was trusted.

Rob Hall understood the relational components of leadership. He knew about *vision*. He knew where he was going. He had stood on the summit of Mount Everest before; in fact, Hall had led thirty-nine climbers to the top of Everest over the past few years. He knew precisely what he had to do to reach his objective – for his clients and for his company. And it was a *shared vision*. When his climbers paid their fees, they accepted ownership and responsibility for that vision. They were ready to live and, it turns out, die for that vision. They had a shared vision, but they made mistakes in the pursuit of that vision. And mountains are not forgiving.

Rob Hall also knew about *values*. He understood teamwork and cooperation even as he competed with the other expeditions. He knew how to care for his people. He gave them their $65,000 worth. He worked for their safety and health first; the summiting of Everest second. He understood human drive and human dignity. He knew how to manage fear and conflict under pressure. He knew the value of life and of relationships and he drilled the rules of the climbing community into his people. They shared these values and agreed to be accountable to live by them. Unfortunately, they did not always follow them. Mistakes were made.

Rob Hall also knew about *vulnerability*. He understood the risk of roping to another person and exposing himself to that person's weaknesses as well as his or her strengths. He knew that the shared vision and the shared values were only as strong as the weakest person on the mountain. A mistake on their team could take down others. An injury on another team could direct time and attention away from their own mission if rescue became necessary. He knew that mistakes, bad judgement, poor decisions, physical limits – his or another's – could abort the mission, defeat the vision, even end in tragedy. Climbers are human. People make mistakes. Vulnerability requires forgiveness. On May 10, mistakes were made. Lives were lost.

Rob Hall was an exceptional leader. Did he know where he was going? Unquestionably! Did he know what was important? Absolutely! Did he understand his vulnerability? Of course. Then what went wrong? No one can say with certainty, but it does seem clear that his values, his commitment to his climbers, caused him to stay behind with a stricken climber desperately needing oxygen. In the end, his values killed him. Vulnerable now to a series of questionable decisions, deteriorating weather and a crippled climber, Rob Hall called his wife on his satellite phone and said goodbye. Mistakes happen. And mountains do not forgive.

Vision, values and vulnerability. Three crucial components of leadership. Rob Hall knew this on Mount Everest. Vision expects responsibility; values call for accountability; vulnerability requires forgiveness. Leadership is about vision, values and vulnerability. It is also about responsibility, accountability and forgiveness.

We have talked about vision and values. We have looked at responsibility and accountability. But what about forgiveness? There is very little in the management literature about forgiveness. This may well be the crisis of leadership today. I am becoming increasingly convinced that there can be no leadership without forgiveness. Leadership requires forgiveness, and forgiveness nurtures leadership.

Forgiving leaders

Last year the editor of a weekly newspaper called to ask me to write an article in response to the accusation that there is a crisis in leadership in higher education in Canada. A scholar had noted the number of advertisements for deans and presidents and concluded that there must be crisis. I wrote the article, responding that there might in fact be a crisis but not the one the scholar had imagined. I noted that there was no shortage of opportunities for leadership in higher education as advertised. I also suggested that there was no shortage of capable people ready to serve organizations and work hard for the vision and values of their institutions. But I did acknowledge that leaders do not last long in higher education. In the field of theological education for example, presidents last four years and deans less than three years on average. After eleven years as president, I am considered one of the veterans – a frightening thought! The crisis of leadership, I believe, is a crisis of forgiveness. Leaders are expected to lead without mistakes. There is very little tolerance for error in our organizations, very little acknowledgement of the human limitations of leaders. Organizations want leaders whom they can place before them to bear the burden of decision without error. Errorless leadership is an oxymoron. You may have heard the story of the young executive who sought out the gruff old corporate leader and asked, 'How can I become a great leader like you?' The senior statesman looked at her and said gruffly, 'Two words: Good decisions!' After pondering this wisdom for a minute the young executive asked, 'How do I learn to make good decisions?' The veteran leader paused and responded, 'One word: Experience!' Persisting, the young executive asked, 'But how do I get this experience?' And as you can already guess, the leader turned to her and said, 'Two words: Wrong decisions!' Leaders lead by learning from their mistakes. And leaders develop other leaders by giving the people for whom they are responsible the space to fail and to learn.

Towards the end of my interview with the board at Regent, I was given the opportunity to ask them some questions. I asked, 'What will you do when I fail? I have never been a president before. I will make mistakes. Will you toss me out when I fall on my face or will you dust me off, stand me up and encourage me to try again?' They did not really have an answer for me at the time, but perhaps the pondering of that question is part of the reason I am still there – still leading, still making mistakes, and still learning from them.

Organizations must create a context of forgiveness if they expect to have quality leadership. And leaders must embrace their own vulnerability and offer forgiveness to followers if they want to contribute to that context of forgiveness and nurture the leadership abilities of their people. Forgiveness may be the most important gift an organization can give to its leaders, and the most important gift a leader can give to the people for whom he or she is responsible. Forgiveness offers people the chance to take risks, to learn and to grow in their own leadership within the organization. Leaders need forgiveness given their own vulnerability and it is something they must offer others, even though others' failures increase the leaders' vulnerability.

Forgiving ourselves

But there is one more thread in this tapestry of leadership, vulnerability and forgiveness. *Leaders must be able to forgive themselves.* This may be the hardest of all. All of us are haunted by the foolish things we have done, the mistakes we have made, the failures of yesterday. Our ability to lead is directly proportional to our ability to forgive ourselves and risk failure again. If our actions are circumscribed by fear of failure, we cannot lead. Failure must be forgiven and learned from. And there is no one harder to forgive than oneself.

In 1928 General Umberto Nobile led an Italian expedition to the North Pole. With the famed explorer Finn Malgrem, Nobile and his men flew the airship *Italia* from Kongs Fjord in the Norwegian Arctic to the North Pole. The expedition succeeded in reaching the Pole but ended in a tragedy similar to the Everest expeditions of 1996.

In 1969 this story was told by Hollywood in a dramatic feature film *The Red Tent*, starring Peter Finch, Sean Connery and Claudia Cardinale. I use this film in my leadership class at Regent. Though nearly thirty years old, the film is still dramatic and engaging, and it is all about leadership. A court sat in judgement on Nobile's leadership, and now all the witnesses are conjured up again in Nobile's mind as he looks back on the expedition as an old man. In his fantasy Nobile reviews the story through the eyes of each of its characters as he seeks to pass judgement on his leadership and his failure. It is a very powerful film. As I show the movie in class, I stop the film at three critical points where the general must make a decision and ask the class what they would do. At the end, before the summary judgement is given, I stop again and ask the students to assess his leadership. If they truly wrestle with the decisions along the way, they are much less certain how to evaluate him at the end.

From the beginning of the movie Nobile has a vision, a dream, of landing on the North Pole. He is captured by his vision and exudes his sense of purpose at every point. It is contagious and his men are caught up in the pursuit of this vision. I stop the tape and ask my class – as I would ask you: Do you have a vision for what you want to accomplish? For your life? For your organization? For your department? Do you live your vision with such vigour that your people have caught it and share your enthusiasm?

As the movie continues, Nobile and his crew arrive at the North Pole and prepare to land. However, at that moment the weather turns – again like Everest – and he must make a hard decision: does he land and accomplish his mission for his country or does he abort the landing and return to Kings Bay (as Kongs Fjord is referred to in the movie) to guarantee the safety of his men? His second-in-command, Major Zappi, states it clearly: 'A leader's responsibility is to his mission – you must land.' But the explorer Malgrem counters, 'No, a leader's responsibility is always to his men – you must return to King's Bay.' Again, I stop the tape and we decide. Vision or values? What will you do?

General Nobile makes his decision and crashes on the Arctic ice, killing several members of his expedition. Huddled on the ice in a red tent, the story becomes a chilling tale of survival, heroism and rescue, with more critical decisions for the general. In the end Nobile is judged for the decisions he makes. But the judgement of history does not haunt him. It is Nobile who cannot forgive himself. Forty years later he is still having nightmares about that trip, about his leadership, about his failures. Only when he faces this harsh reality in a poignant and powerful conclusion can he admit his failure, affirm his accomplishment, accept the judgement of history on his leadership, forgive himself and sleep again.

This is a powerful movie about the vision, values and vulnerability of leadership; a strong statement about the critical relationship between leadership and forgiveness. Relational leadership is a risky business. We are entrusted with a vision; we are entrusted with the dreams and gifts and hopes of the people. We are accountable to God and to the organization. We will fail and others will fail us. Without the hope of forgiveness, we would never have the courage to take up leadership – to offer ourselves as servants of the shared vision and the shared values of our organizations. Without forgiveness, we would never commit ourselves to the interdependent relationships of our communities. But forgiveness comes with the gift of leadership. It is the empowering side of accountability. And forgiveness flows from the heart of the leader's relationship with God.

Conclusion: Prayer and Benediction

As you take up the responsibilities of leadership, as you give yourself in the service of the people whom God has entrusted to your care, as you join them in the pursuit of a shared vision and shared values, as you surround organizational mission with community life, I pray with Paul and Jude:

asking God to fill you with the knowledge of his will through all spiritual wisdom and understanding ... that you may live a life worthy of the Lord and may please him in every way: bearing fruit in every good work, growing in the knowledge of God, being strengthened with all power according to his glorious might so that you may have great endurance and patience, and joyfully giving thanks to the Father, who has qualified you to share in the inheritance of the saints in the kingdom of light. For he has rescued us from the dominion of darkness and brought us into the kingdom of the Son he loves, in whom we have redemption, the forgiveness of sins. (Col 1:9–14)

To him who is able to keep you from falling and to present you before his glorious presence without fault and with great joy – to the only God our Saviour be glory, majesty, power and authority, through Jesus Christ our Lord, before all ages, now and forevermore! Amen. (Jude 24–25)

Notes

[1] Dietrich Bonhoeffer, 'The Nazi Rise to Power', *No Rusty Swords* (New York: Harper & Row, 1965), 190–204.
[2] Ann McGee Cooper, *Time Management for Unmanageable People* (New York: Bantam Books, 1994), 21.
[3] Cooper, *Time*, 25.
[4] Cooper, *Time*, 25–28.
[5] Cooper, *Time*, 29.
[6] Cooper, *Time*, 41.

Index

Introductory Note

Entries for book and journal titles are shown in italics, and references to notes are given in parentheses following the page number, eg 114(n3).